Developing Science

DEVELOPING SCIENTIFIC SKILLS AND KNOWLEDGE

year

6

Christine Moorcroft

Contents

Introduction   4

Notes on the activities   5

Interdependence and adaptation

Dark to light   14
Understanding that green plants make new plant
material using air and water in the presence of light

Plant key: plants   15
Using keys to identify plants

Plant key: questions   16
Using keys to identify plants

Pond food web   17
Understanding that animals and plants in a
habitat are interdependent

Your web   18
Understanding that food chains can be used to
represent feeding relationships in a habitat

Soil match   19
Understanding that different plants grow in
different soil conditions

Fertilisers   20
Recognising that fertilisers are often added to soils
to provide plants with the nutrients they need

The seashore   21
Understanding that different animals and plants
are found in different habitats

Habitat watch   22
Understanding how animals and plants in a
habitat are suited to their environment

Micro-organisms

A question of illness   23
Understanding that there are very small organisms
called micro-organisms which can be harmful

Mouldy matters   24
Understanding that micro-organisms are often too
small to be seen and can cause food to decay

Barbecue bugs   25
Recognising that food needs to be handled and
stored with care

A lot of rot   26
Understanding that living micro-organisms bring
about decay, which can be beneficial

A vital ingredient
Understanding that micro-organisms feed

Yummy yogurt   28
Recognising that micro-organisms are useful in
food production

More about dissolving

Clean up   29
Understanding that solids which do not dissolve in
water can be separated from it by filtering

What's in it?   30
Recognising that when solids dissolve in water a
clear solution is formed

Steamy stuff   31
Making and testing predictions about water
containing dissolved materials

'Frosted' glass   32
Understanding that when the liquid evaporates
from a solution the solid is left behind

Quick dissolvers   33
Turning ideas into a fair test

Dissolving time   34
Understanding that several repeated measurements
provide data that can be used with more confidence

Speed it up   35
Turning ideas about helping solids to dissolve more
quickly into a form that can be investigated

Graph it   36
Using a graph to present results

Reversible and irreversible changes

Mix it up   37
Recognising that mixing materials can cause
them to change

Time for a change   38
Making careful observations, recording and
explaining these using scientific knowledge

Sherbet fizz   39
Recognising that mixing materials can cause
them to change

Hot and cold   40
Recognising that heating or cooling causes
some materials to change

Burn up   41
Recognising that when materials are burned,
new materials are formed

Candlelight   42
...changes that occur when
...urned are not reversible

Forces in action

Measure the force   43
Understanding that weight is a force and is
measured in newtons

All kinds of forces   44
Recognising that several forces may act
on one object

Floating forces   45
Recognising that when an object is submerged in
water, the water provides an upward force on it

Check it   46
Repeating measurements to check them;
evaluating repeated measures

It's elastic   47
Understanding that how much an elastic band
stretches depends on the force acting on it

Air force   48
Understanding that air resistance slows
moving objects

How we see things

Beam blocker   49
Recognising that light travels from a source

Now you see it   50
Understanding that we see light sources because
light from the source enters our eyes

Target practice   51
Recognising that light from an object can be
reflected by a mirror

Beam tracer   52
Indicating the direction of a beam or ray of light
travelling from a light source by a straight line
with an arrowhead

Enlarge it   53
Identifying factors that might affect the size and
position of the shadow of an object

Shadows and reflections   54
Recognising the difference between shadows
and 'reflections'

Changing circuits

Who's there?   55
Reviewing previous learning about electric circuits

Circuit diagrams   56
Recognising that there are conventional symbols
for components in circuits and that these can
be used to draw diagrams of circuits

Wired up   57
Understanding that the brightness of bulbs in a
circuit can be changed

Wire wise   58
Understanding that the brightness of bulbs in a
circuit can be changed by changing the wires

Dim it   59
Explaining observations in terms of knowledge
about electrical circuits

Enquiry in environmental and technological contexts

Tilt switch   60
Using scientific knowledge to identify significant
features of an artefact to be designed

Alarm   61
Planning a suitable approach to a design

Pressure pad   62
Using scientific knowledge to identify significant
features of an artefact to be designed

Switch test   63
Testing and trying to explain designs using scientific
knowledge and understanding

Trial log   64
Evaluating the limitations of one's own and
others' designs

Reprinted 2006, 2007
Published 2004 by A & C Black Publishers Limited
38 Soho Square, London W1D 3HB
www.acblack.com

ISBN 978-0-7136-6645-8

The author and publishers would like to thank Catherine Yemm,
Trevor Davies and the staff of Balsall Common Primary School
for their assistance in producing this series of books.

A CIP catalogue record for this book is available
from the British Library.

Printed in Great Britain by St Edmundsbury Press Ltd,
Bury St Edmunds, Suffolk.

A & C Black uses paper produced with elemental chlorine-
free pulp, harvested from managed sustainable forests.

Developing Science is a series of seven photocopiable activity books to support the teaching of science. Each book provides a range of activities that not only develop children's knowledge and understanding of science, but also provide opportunities to develop their scientific skills: planning experimental work, and obtaining and considering evidence.

The activities vary in their approach: some are based on first-hand observations, some present the findings of investigations for the children to analyse and others require the children to find information from books and electronic sources. They focus on different parts of a scientific investigation: questioning, responding to questions, generating ideas, planning, predicting, carrying out a fair test or an investigation, recording findings, checking and questioning findings, explaining findings and presenting explanations.

The activities in **Year 6** are based on Science in the National Curriculum and the QCA scheme of work for Year 6. They provide opportunities for the children to:

- develop curiosity about the things they observe and experience, and explore the world about them with all their senses;
- use this experience to develop their understanding of key scientific ideas and make links between different phenomena and experiences;
- begin to think about models to represent things they cannot directly experience;
- try to make sense of phenomena, seeking explanations and thinking critically about claims and ideas;
- acquire and refine the practical skills needed to investigate questions safely;
- develop skills of predicting, asking questions, making inferences, concluding and evaluating (based on evidence and understanding), and to use these skills in investigative work;
- practise mathematical skills such as counting, ordering numbers, measuring using standard and non-standard measures, and recording and interpreting simple charts;
- learn why numerical and mathematical skills are useful and helpful to understanding;
- think creatively about science and enjoy trying to make sense of phenomena;
- develop language skills through talking about their work and presenting their own ideas, using systematic writing of different kinds;
- use scientific and mathematical language (including technical vocabulary and conventions) and to draw pictures, diagrams and charts to communicate scientific ideas;
- read non-fiction and extract information from sources such as reference books or CD-ROMs;
- work with others, listening to their ideas and treating these with respect;
- develop respect for evidence and evaluate critically ideas which may or may not fit the evidence available;
- develop a respect for the environment and living things and for their own health and safety.

The activities are carefully linked with the National Literacy Strategy to give the children opportunities to develop their reading skills in finding information (for example, scanning a text and reading instructions) and to use a range of writing skills in presenting their findings (for example, making notes and writing reports). Science-related vocabulary to introduce is provided in the **Notes on the activities** on pages 5–13.

Teachers are encouraged to introduce the activities presented in this book in a stimulating classroom environment that provides facilities for the children to explore the topics to be covered: for example, through the provision of materials, equipment, pictures, books and electronic resources connected with subjects such as habitats and food chains, gravity and resistance, and electrical circuits.

Each activity sheet specifies the learning objective and has a **Teachers' note** at the foot of the page, which you may wish to mask before photocopying. Expanded teaching notes are provided in the **Notes on the activities**. Most activities end with a challenge (**Now try this!**) which reinforces and extends the children's learning and provides the teacher with an opportunity for assessment. These extension activities might be appropriate for only a few children; it is not expected that the whole class should complete them. A notebook or separate sheet of paper will be required for the children to complete the extension activities.

Health and safety

Developing Science recognises the importance of safety in science lessons and provides advice on the ways in which teachers can make their lessons as safe as possible (including links to useful websites). The books also suggest ways in which to encourage children to take appropriate responsibility for their own safety. Teachers are recommended to follow the safety guidelines provided in the QCA scheme of work or in *Be Safe!* (available from the Association for Science Education – see their website, www.ase.org.uk). Specific health and safety advice is included in the **Notes on the activities** and warnings to the children feature on the activity sheets where relevant.

Online resources

In addition to the photocopiable activity sheets in this book, a collection of online science resources is available on the A & C Black website at www.acblack.com/developingscience. These activities can be used either as stand-alone teaching resources or in conjunction with the printed sheets. An (ICT) icon on an activity page indicates that there is a resource on the website specifically designed to complement that activity. The website tasks have been designed to provide experiences that are not easy to reproduce in the classroom: for example, observing a variety of habitats and finding out about the effects of micro-organisms on humans.

The notes below expand upon those provided at the foot of the activity pages. They give ideas for making the most of the activity sheet, including suggestions for the whole-class introduction, the plenary session or for follow-up work using an adapted version of the activity sheet. To help teachers to select appropriate learning experiences for their pupils, the activities are grouped into sections within each book, but the pages need not be presented in the order in which they appear unless stated otherwise. Where appropriate, links to other areas of the curriculum are indicated, in particular to literacy and numeracy.

Interdependence and adaptation

This section builds on **Helping plants grow well** from **Year 3**, **Habitats** from **Year 4** and **Keeping healthy** from **Year 5**.

Dark to light (page 14) helps the children to learn that green plants need light in order to grow well and that they use air and water to produce new plant material, but that this process can be carried out only in the

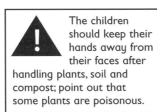

The children should keep their hands away from their faces after handling plants, soil and compost; point out that some plants are poisonous.

presence of light. You could begin by asking the children to bring in the labels or care instructions from house plants and asking them to work in groups to compare the needs of different plants. Ask them to notice what all plants need. Show them a plant that has been kept in the dark for a week or two and ask them what is wrong with it. Discuss how the plant can be helped back to health, and what changes will be seen when it is healthy: for example, the leaves will be green, new leaves might appear and the stem should be stronger. Geranium and busy lizzy, or a tray of grass, are suitable for this. Discuss why plants need light: point out that they make their own food using chemicals in their leaves, air and light, but that they cannot do this well without light. You could introduce the term *photosynthesis* for the process through which plants produce their food. A few plants, such as the bog-growing Venus fly-trap, sundew, butterwort and pitcher plant, are rooted in sphagnum moss, not soil; they do not take in all the nutrients they need through their roots and obtain these by trapping and digesting small animals such as flies.

Vocabulary: *light, growth, photosynthesis, produce, strength.*

Plant key: plants and **Plant key: questions** (pages 15–16) help the children to use keys to identify plants and to make their own keys. They should already have had the opportunity to observe plants at first hand and to notice the differences between them: for example, the sizes and shapes of leaves, arrangements of leaves, whether or not the leaves are serrated, the colour, size and shape of the flowers and how they are arranged. Encourage them to add others to the key, especially those that are similar to some of these, and to look for differences; for example, oilseed rape and ragwort have similarities in appearance with groundsel and feverfew (small flowers arranged with many small petals radiating from a central point). Encourage them to look for differences between similar-looking plants. Introduce vocabulary to help the children to describe the plants: for

example, *umbel* (a group of small flowers on a stalk that comes from the same central point as other similar stalks: for example, in hogweed and cow parsley), *spire* (a tall stem with flowers growing along its length, as in rosebay willowherb, white dead nettle and foxglove). The children could play 'Guess who?' in pairs: each child needs a copy of the page and Player 1 needs a copy from which all the pictures have been cut into separate cards. Player 1 chooses a flower and Player 2 has to work out which it is by asking questions that eliminate the others (he or she could cover the eliminated plants with slips of paper). The questions on page 16 could be used; they must be answered by Yes or No. Higher-attaining children could use the questions and pictures to create a key. The plants chosen are ones that the children might have seen but are unlikely to know well. In literacy lessons, the children could compile a list of plant names that are compound words (for example, *cornflower, hogweed*) and look up the derivations of some plant names.

Resources: information books with pictures of plants

Vocabulary: *columbine, cornflower, cow parsley, feverfew, fumitory, groundsel (chickweed), hogweed, serrated, spire, tufted vetch, umbel, white dead nettle.*

Pond food web and **Your web** (pages 17–18) develop the children's understanding of the interdependence of animals and plants in a habitat, and reinforce their understanding that animals have to find their food whereas plants produce their own. You could introduce the terms *consumers* for animals and *producers* for plants.

Vocabulary: *consumer, eat, feed, food web, habitat, nutrients, producer.*

Soil match (page 19) helps the children to learn why plants grow well in different places and develops their understanding of how plants feed (in addition to producing food from the air around them in the presence of light, they take in nutrients and

Point out that some plants are poisonous. The children should keep their hands away from their faces when handling plants and soil and should wash their hands afterwards.

water through their roots). Different groups could grow different plants in each type of soil. Use the plants listed under **Resources** – or any you might have available. The children might find that some plants grow equally well in any soil. Discuss why a bar chart is suitable: it is a good way to record height. Link this with numeracy (handling data). You could also begin a poster of poisonous plants to which the children contribute as they find out about them.

Resources: plant seeds: for example, campanula, nemesia and petunia (grow well in chalky soil); aubretia, helianthemum, poppy, salvia and scabious (grow well in sandy soil); aquilegia, dicentra, hosta and rudbeckia (grow well in clay soil); and geranium (grows well in sandy and clay soils) • chalky, sandy and clay soils • pots or seed trays • small trowels or large old spoons

Vocabulary: *chalk, clay, nutrients, sand, soil type.*

Fertilisers (page 20) reinforces the children's knowledge that water and nutrients are taken in through the roots of plants. It also helps them to learn about the ways in which

 Point out that some plants are poisonous. The children should keep their hands away from their faces when handling plants and soil and should wash their hands afterwards.

animals and plants are suited to their habitats, that different plants grow well in different soil conditions and that soil quality can be improved by the addition of fertilisers.

Vocabulary: *feed, fertiliser, nutrients, produce, roots, water.*

The seashore (page 21) helps the children to understand why different animals are found in different habitats and how they are suited to their environment. Herring gulls feed on fish and build their nests on ledges on cliffs. The herring gull also eats shellfish; it drops them onto rocks to break their shells. The sea anemone catches small aquatic animals with its tentacles. The shore crab, sand eel, sand smelt, sea anemone and barnacle need to be in salt water to survive. The sand eel burrows into the sand beneath the water if it is alarmed. Barnacles attach themselves to rocks and build a hard wall around themselves using a substance they produce. The sand smelt lays its eggs on seaweed. To provide links with literacy the children could compile a mini-encyclopedia of seashore animals.

Vocabulary: *barnacle, habitat, herring gull, sand eel, sand smelt, sea anemone, shore crab.*

ICT **Habitat watch** (page 22) helps the children to understand why different animals and plants are found in different habitats and how animals and plants in a habitat are suited to their environment. You could ask the children if they think the plant or animal would survive in a completely different habitat, with questions such as 'Could a frog live on a beach?', 'Could a water lily grow in a dry field?', 'Could a tadpole live in a desert?' Ask the children to explain their answers; this will help them to identify the conditions that make habitats suitable for different animals or plants. A complementary activity for this sheet is available on the website (see Year 6 Activity 1).

Micro-organisms

The activities in this section build on **Teeth and eating** from **Year 3** and **Interdependence and adaptation** (see above).

A question of illness (page 23) develops the children's understanding about the very small organisms called micro-organisms that can be harmful and about the

 This work should be carried out in accordance with the school's policy on personal, social and health education.

sources of scientific ideas about diseases. You could begin by discussing common illnesses such as colds, stomach upsets, food poisoning, chickenpox, influenza and cuts that become infected. Explain that when part of the body becomes infected in any way it is because micro-organisms have entered it and are living there and breeding. Point out that the body produces materials to fight the micro-organisms but that sometimes it needs the help of medicines.

Resources: information books • leaflets from pharmacies and health centres • electronic sources about common illnesses and their causes, such as *Encyclopedia Britannica* CD-ROM, *Become A Human Body Explorer* CD-ROM (Dorling Kindersley), BBCi Health website (www.bbc.co.uk/health)

Vocabulary: *bacterium* (plural *bacteria*), *germ, illness, micro-organism, organism, virus.*

Mouldy matters (page 24) helps the children to learn that micro-organisms, which are usually too small to be seen, can cause food to decay. Discuss how decaying food can be observed safely and display the

 Mouldy foods should be kept in sealed containers such as clear plastic boxes or bags so that the children can look at them without handling them.

agreed rules. After the children have looked at some mouldy food, ask them what has caused the mould. Link this with their existing experience by asking them where and when they have seen mouldy food and what they think made it go mouldy. Does old food always go mouldy? Discuss the conditions that cause mould. The children could compare what happens to a piece of bread that is left uncovered in a dry place with another one kept in a plastic bag; they could also compare similar foods kept in a fridge and in a freezer. Encourage them to deduce what helps mould to grow and what helps to prevent it. Link this to the ways in which food is treated to keep it fresh: for example, drying, refrigerating, freezing, salting and canning. Explain that mould is produced by the action of micro-organisms on food and that these micro-organisms can live and breed only between certain temperatures. The children could find out about the temperatures at which foods are stored in supermarkets and consider why this is. Micro-organisms need food, warmth and water in order to survive.

Resources: mouldy bread, fruit and cheese in sealed plastic bags or boxes • magnifying glasses

Vocabulary: *bacteria, breed, micro-organism, mould.*

ICT **Barbecue bugs** (page 25) develops the children's understanding about the micro-organisms that can cause food to decay and about the need to handle and store food with care. It is useful to point out that food does not change of its own accord but that the action of micro-organisms changes it. Micro-organisms are present in the air; they can also be transferred to food from other places by flies and other insects. There are micro-organisms in raw meat – these are destroyed by cooking, but can be transferred to food that has been cooked or is to be eaten raw. This can be avoided by using different utensils for raw meat and for cooked food or raw foods such as salads. If possible, arrange a visit to a local establishment where food is prepared or ask the school cook to talk to the children about hygiene in the school kitchen. Provide information books, leaflets and posters about food hygiene (the children can also look for food hygiene information in Internet sources). Link this with literacy skills: writing instructions and recognising and using imperative verb forms. A complementary activity for this sheet is available on the website (see Year 6 Activity 2).

Resources: information books, posters and leaflets on food hygiene • a computer

Vocabulary: *bacteria, germ, hygiene, micro-organism.*

A lot of rot (page 26) helps the children to learn that micro-organisms, which are living organisms, bring about decay, and that this decay can be beneficial. You could first take the children out to look for rotting materials in the neighbourhood: fences, window frames, compost, leaves and so on. Ask them to describe the ways in which the materials have changed and to say what they think makes them rot. Encourage the use of comparative forms of adjectives learned during literacy lessons. Record the children's responses. Ask them what they notice about the types of materials that rot (they are from living organisms – plants and animals). Discuss what would happen if dead plant and animal material did not rot and point out that micro-organisms are helpful in destroying waste material. Children who live in rural areas might be familiar with the ways in which animal waste is used as a fertiliser and might know about septic tanks in which human waste is treated by the action of micro-organisms. They could also find out about how the local water authority deals with sewage, using micro-organisms.

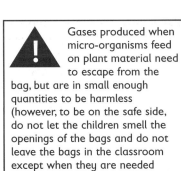 Gases produced when micro-organisms feed on plant material need to escape from the bag, but are in small enough quantities to be harmless (however, to be on the safe side, do not let the children smell the openings of the bags and do not leave the bags in the classroom except when they are needed for observation).

Resources: clear plastic bags • grass cuttings or leaves • wire closures

Vocabulary: *bacteria, gases, germ, micro-organism, organism, safety.*

A vital ingredient (page 27) helps the children to learn that micro-organisms are living things that feed and grow. It encourages them to make suggestions about what yeast needs in order to feed and grow, to make careful observations

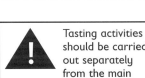 Tasting activities should be carried out separately from the main investigation and in hygienic conditions. Do not remove the balloons from the plastic bottles containing yeast.

and to compare these in order to draw conclusions about the effect of yeast on dough. They are also given the opportunity to explain conclusions using their scientific knowledge and understanding. The children should find that the yeast mixture that contains sugar and warm water increases in size more than the others and becomes bubbly; the balloon inflates slightly because of the gases produced (mainly carbon dioxide). Help the children to link this with the action of yeast on bread: while the yeast is in warm conditions it increases in size, especially if it is mixed with sugar (on which it feeds), but once it is cooked it stops doing so. This is because yeast is a fungus that needs warmth and water in order to live and breed, but very hot conditions kill it. Fresh yeast can be frozen or refrigerated; these do not kill it but render it dormant. Dried yeast is dormant because of the lack of water. Emphasise that this is a situation in which micro-organisms are helpful rather than harmful. Other foods in whose production micro-organisms are used include yogurt, tea, beer, wine and cheese. You could also discuss other fungi with which the children are familiar, such as mushrooms. Scientists do not distinguish between toadstools and mushrooms but in everyday terms the word *toadstool* is generally used for harmful mushrooms. Scientists now classify fungi as living organisms that are neither animals nor plants. You could link this with the children's previous learning about plants; plants produce their own food from the air around them in the presence of light (see notes for **Dark to light** on page 5), but fungi feed on other materials.

Resources: dried yeast • sugar • warm water • small, clear plastic bottles • small round balloons • teaspoons

Vocabulary: *fungus* (plural *fungi*), *gases, micro-organism, mushroom, organism, toadstool, yeast.*

Yummy yogurt (page 28) develops the children's understanding of the useful action of micro-organisms on foods. It allows them to make careful observations and compare these in order to draw conclusions, and to explain conclusions using scientific knowledge and understanding. The bacteria (Lactobacilli, usually L. Bulgaricus or L. Acidophilus) are usually referred to as a *culture*. At room temperature they change the consistency and taste of milk, producing yogurt. 'Live' yogurt contains living bacteria but yogurt that is not 'live' has been heated, killing the bacteria after they have altered the milk. The children could add fruit juice or chopped fruit to the yogurt before they refrigerate it. They could also try making yogurt using non-live yogurt and observe what happens.

 Encourage the children to devise their own hygiene rules for handling foods. Ensure that all equipment and hands are clean. It is best to use sterilised equipment for yogurt-making. Use a proprietary sterilising solution. Check that none of the children has a milk allergy if they are to eat the yogurt.

Resources: milk • natural yogurt • natural live yogurt • saucepan • cooker top • wide-necked flask or insulated jar • tablespoons • measuring jugs • whisk • fridge

Vocabulary: *bacteria, bacterium, culture, micro-organism, organism, sterilise, yogurt.*

More about dissolving

The activities in this section build on **Solids, liquids and how they can be separated** from **Year 4** and **Gases around us** from **Year 5**.

Clean up (page 29) develops the children's knowledge and understanding about solids that do not dissolve in water and can be separated from it by filtering, which is similar to sieving. They develop skills in describing a scientific process. You could begin by visiting a water treatment

 Ensure that the children keep their hands away from their faces during their work and wash their hands after handling dirty water. Ensure that they understand that, although the filtered water looks clean, it is not pure enough to drink because it might contain micro-organisms.

plant or the Environment Agency website to find out how drinking water is purified. The children could pour the water through filter paper (in a funnel) or through fine gravel or sand (in a piece of muslin tied across the top of a jar or other container).

Resources: small clear plastic pots or jars • water containing mud and gravel • filter papers • funnels • fine gravel • sand • fine cloth such as muslin

Vocabulary: *clean, dissolve, filter, purified, purify, separate, sieve.*

What's in it? (page 30) revises the children's previous learning about separating solids from liquids and about dissolving. They learn that when solids dissolve in water a clear solution is formed (which may be coloured) and that the solid cannot be separated by filtering; also that when the

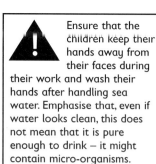

Ensure that the children keep their hands away from their faces during their work and wash their hands after handling sea water. Emphasise that, even if water looks clean, this does not mean that it is pure enough to drink – it might contain micro-organisms.

liquid evaporates from a solution the solid remains. They also have the opportunity to make predictions about which liquids contain dissolved materials and to test these predictions. They have already separated undissolved material from water (page 29); ask them if they think any material might remain in the water they filtered. How can they find out? Remind them of their previous learning about dissolved salt (in **Solids, liquids and how they can be separated** in **Year 5**). They can leave small quantities of each liquid in saucers so that the water evaporates, or an adult could heat the liquids to speed up the evaporation of the water. They should find that all the liquids except distilled water contain dissolved material (although some tap water might contain very little dissolved material). Distilled water is water that has evaporated, condensed and been collected in clean containers. This activity requires the children to read and write words with difficult spellings: for example, *separate, dissolved, distilled, solution*. Encourage them to use appropriate spelling strategies.

Resources: filtered water • sea water • tap water • tea • water-based ink • distilled water

Vocabulary: *clean, condense, dissolve, distilled water, evaporate, filter, purified, purify, separate, sieve.*

Steamy stuff (page 31) develops the children's understanding about what happens when the liquid evaporates from a solution (the solid remains). It encourages them to make predictions about what is dissolved in the liquids they observe and to test these

Ensure that the children cannot touch the hotplate or oven top and the saucepan (you could place a small table between the cooker top and the children). Make sure that all utensils are clean when heating salt or sugar solutions so that the children can taste the condensed water.

predictions. The children should be able to predict, from their previous learning, that droplets of water will collect on the cold plate and know that the water comes from the water in the pan, which has been boiled and evaporated. After the children have observed what happens to each liquid, ask them if their predictions were right. Discuss why they were right (or wrong). Did they think the condensed water would contain the material that was dissolved in it? Explain that only the water evaporates; the solid material remains in the saucepan. Explain that the water collected on the plate is distilled water (albeit not as pure as commercially-produced distilled water).

Resources: saucepan • oven glove • cooker top or hotplate • plate • water

Vocabulary: *boil, condensation, condense, dissolve, distilled water, evaporate, liquid, solution, steam.*

'Frosted' glass (page 32) consolidates the children's learning that when the liquid evaporates from a solution the

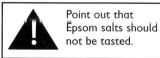

Point out that Epsom salts should not be tasted.

solid remains. It gives them an opportunity to make predictions about what will happen when water containing dissolved materials evaporates, and to test these predictions. The activity is particularly helpful for lower-attaining children. The 'frosted' patterns are the result of evaporated water leaving behind deposits of crystals of Epsom salts and can easily be washed off the windows. Link this activity with literacy: writing explanations.

Resources: water • Epsom salts (hydrated magnesium sulphate) • clear plastic pots • teaspoons • warm water • windows

Vocabulary: *crystal, dissolve, Epsom salts, evaporate, solution.*

Quick dissolvers and **Dissolving time** (pages 33–34) encourage the children to make predictions, turn ideas into a fair test and make

Point out that this is not a tasting activity.

careful observations and measurements; to make comparisons and draw conclusions. **Dissolving time** also provides a graph on which to represent the results of their investigations. Revise their previous learning about dissolving and ensure that they understand that a material has dissolved when it can no longer be seen in the water. The children might need help in thinking of a way in which to measure which sugar dissolves the most quickly. They could count the number of times they stir it or they could time it. For a fair test they should keep the water temperature and quantities of sugar and water the same. If they are timing it they should stir each sugar the same number of times. Discuss how they will keep one teaspoon dry for spooning out sugar (by using a different one for stirring).

Resources: granulated sugar • demerara sugar • caster sugar • icing sugar • sugar cubes • teaspoons • clear plastic pots • water

Vocabulary: *dissolve, graph, repeat, solution.*

Speed it up and **Graph it** (pages 35–36) help the children to turn ideas about dissolving into a form that can be investigated and to represent their results on a graph. Link page 36 with work in numeracy: measurement and handling data.

Resources: sugar • teaspoons • clear plastic pots • thermometers • timers or stopwatches • water

Vocabulary: *disappear, evaporate, gas, water vapour.*

Reversible and irreversible changes

The activities in this section build on **Grouping and changing materials** from **Year 2**, **Changing state** from **Year 5** and **More about dissolving** (see above). Some of these activities involve heating and burning materials using candles or nightlights. If your school's health and safety policy forbids this, ask someone to make a video recording of you carrying out demonstration activities elsewhere, and show these to the pupils at the appropriate times.

Mix it up (page 37) develops the children's understanding of the behaviour of mixtures; they compare mixtures in which materials are changed, making new

An adult should handle the cement; it is best to wear plastic gloves since cement contains lime, which can irritate the skin. The other materials are safe to handle but must not be tasted.

materials, with those in which the mixtures can be separated. They are encouraged to make careful observations, record them and explain what they observed. Link this with literacy: words ending in *-able* and *-ible*. Ask the children to predict which materials will dissolve and to say how they know. If a material dissolves in water no particles are visible. Give the children small amounts (two or three teaspoonfuls) of each material so that they do not add too much to the water, because there is a limit to the amount of solid that can dissolve in a set amount of water (the solution becomes *saturated* – it will not take any more solid). After the children have mixed the materials ask them to hold the plastic pots to see if they can feel any change in temperature; plaster of Paris becomes very warm as it sets because of the chemical reaction that is taking place.

Resources: clear plastic pots • plastic spoons • water • Andrews salts • baking powder • cement • cornflour • Epsom salts • flour • plaster of Paris • powder paint • sand • tea leaves or the contents of teabags

Vocabulary: *change, chemical, dissolve, mixture, reaction, reversible, saturated.*

Time for a change (page 38) reviews the children's understanding of some of the changes that can happen when materials are mixed and form new materials. It encourages

An adult should handle the cement; it is best to wear plastic gloves since cement contains lime, which can irritate the skin. The other materials are safe to handle but must not be tasted.

them to make careful observations, to record them and explain what happened, using scientific knowledge and understanding. The following can be separated by filtering: sand and water, tea leaves and water; the following can be separated by evaporating the water: salt and water, sugar and water. In the following, new materials are made and so they cannot be separated: plaster of Paris and water, Epsom salts and water, cement and water. It may appear to the children that Epsom salts can be separated from water by evaporation; discuss what they observed happening: they should have seen bubbles. Ask the children what bubbles contain (air, or a gas of some kind). Where did the gas come from? Point out that when Epsom salts and water are mixed, a gas is formed and this escapes into the air. When the gas is formed it uses up an ingredient of Epsom salts, and so the Epsom salts are changed. The children could test this by evaporating the water from the mixture and then mixing the reclaimed solid with water. Does it still fizz? Flour and water appear to be separated by filtering but if the solid that has been separated is left to dry, it is not quite the same as the original flour because some of the ingredients of flour dissolve in water but others do not. This can be demonstrated by weighing the flour before mixing it with water and comparing this with the weight of the reclaimed, dried solid. In the extension activity, sand can be separated from salt and water by filtering; the remaining salt can then be separated by evaporating the water. If evaporation is carried out first, it is difficult to separate sand and salt. Salt, sugar and water cannot easily be separated. Point out to the children that

because no new material has been made, it is possible to separate them using the right equipment. This applies to any mixture where no new material is made.

Resources: clear plastic pots • plastic spoons • cement • cornflour • Epsom salts • flour • plaster of Paris • sand • salt • tea leaves or the contents of teabags

Vocabulary: *change, dissolve, evaporate, gas, irreversible, liquid, mixture, reversible, separate.*

Sherbet fizz (page 39) develops the children's awareness that mixing materials can cause them to change. They are encouraged to make careful observations, to record them and explain what happened, using scientific knowledge and understanding.

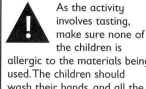

As the activity involves tasting, make sure none of the children is allergic to the materials being used. The children should wash their hands, and all the equipment must be clean.

After the children have completed the activity and mixed the sherbet with water, discuss what their findings tell them about whether or not a new material has been made (the bubbles). If a new material has been made the materials cannot be separated. This is an irreversible change. The children could also try mixing sodium bicarbonate with water but no citric acid and observe (but not necessarily taste) what happens. Carbon dioxide gas is produced when sodium bicarbonate is mixed with an acid: for example, vinegar, lemon juice or orange juice. Baking powder already contains an acid, and so it fizzes (produces a gas) in water without the need to add an acid. Food quality citric acid can be bought from chemists. Tell the children that some acids are dangerous but that many foods contain acids like citric acid. They might be able to name some acid-tasting foods (vinegar, orange juice, lemon juice, apple, grape).

Resources: beaker • citric acid crystals • icing sugar • sodium bicarbonate • teaspoon

Vocabulary: *conditions, evaporate, gas, liquid, measurement, observation, prediction.*

Hot and cold (page 40) develops the children's understanding about the changes that occur when materials are heated and when they are cooled. These are all changes that the children should have observed at school or at home, but you could set up a demonstration for the children to observe if necessary. It is useful to remind the children of the changes they observed when cement, Epsom salts, Andrews salts and plaster of Paris were mixed with water (new materials were formed and so the changes were irreversible).

Vocabulary: *cool, evaporate, gas, heat, irreversible, liquid, reversible, solid.*

ICT Burn up (page 41) helps the children to learn that when materials are burned new materials are formed. Encourage them to talk about their everyday experience of things that burn: for example, from barbecues, bonfires, coal, oil or log fires and stoves at home, and cooking. You could show the children the remains of a bonfire (set this up elsewhere and bring in the cooled remains). Include partly-burned wood, paper, plastic, card and different fabrics as well as metal items that have been in a fire. After the children have observed the materials, discuss the changes. It is useful to weigh a piece of wood before and after burning to show that it becomes lighter. Ask the children what has happened. If the wood has become lighter something must have gone from it. Where has the missing material gone to? Ask the children if the changes are reversible, and how they can tell. They should notice that the material is different after burning and that, if it has changed from solid to liquid (and solidified when cool) as in the case of plastic, the new material is different from the original. The changes are irreversible. A complementary activity for this sheet is available on the website (see Year 6 Activity 3).

Discuss how to observe the burning materials safely, as described in the warning box on page 41. Use a very small piece of each material in case any gases are produced when it burns. Discuss how to put out accidental small fires: by removing the air supply (covering with water or sand or smothering them with thick cloth or even newspaper).

Resources: *Either:* a video showing materials burning *or:* a nightlight • a metal tray containing sand • matches • tongs or clothes pegs • a collection of materials to burn, such as a twig, cotton, wool and polyester fabric, polythene, metal, paper, foil, card, dry grass and newly-cut grass

> **Vocabulary:** *burn, change of state, gas, heat, irreversible, liquid, reversible, solid.*

Candlelight (page 42) helps the children to learn that when materials are burned a new material is sometimes formed. They may predict that the changes are reversible because they know that materials which melt when hot become solid when cooled, and that changes of state are reversible. When a candle *burns*, however, a flame is produced. Energy is needed to produce the heat; this energy uses the wax of the candle as a fuel. A gas is produced from the candle wax during burning. Because of these changes the wax becomes lighter, because materials have been used to produce energy. You could compare this with what happens when wood, paper, fabrics or coal burn. The change is not reversible.

Resources: candle • matches • Plasticine • ruler • scales • sand in a foil dish

> **Vocabulary:** *dry up, evaporate, factor, fair test, gas, liquid.*

Forces in action

The activities in this section build on **Magnets and springs** from **Year 3** and **Friction** from **Year 4**.

Measure the force (page 43) develops the children's understanding that the Earth and objects are pulled towards one another by a force called gravity and that this pull gives objects weight.

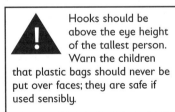

Hooks should be above the eye height of the tallest person. Warn the children that plastic bags should never be put over faces; they are safe if used sensibly.

It helps them to begin to understand that weight is a force, measured in newtons, and practises numeracy skills: making and recording measurements. To help the children to use the forcemeter accurately, hang it from a cup hook screwed into a shelf (above eye height). The hook is likely to be too high for the children to read the scale: tie a loop of string through the handle of the forcemeter and hang the string from the hook.

Emphasise that the weight suspended from the forcemeter is pulled downwards by gravity. Note: mass is measured in grams or kilograms. It is the 'amount of stuff' something is made of; it does not change if the pull of gravity changes (for example, astronauts have the same mass in space or on the Moon as they do on Earth, but their weight changes, because weight is a force – measured in newtons – which is affected by gravity).

Resources: forcemeters with different scales • plastic bags • objects to weigh (such as stones, bricks, shoes, books, pencil cases, coats, jumpers, pencils)

> **Vocabulary:** *force, forcemeter, gravity, pull.*

All kinds of forces (page 44) helps the children to learn about the different forces that can act on objects. They are asked to look at pictures of forces in action and to note what causes each force. The forces in the pictures are: magnetism pulling the pin (the pin is also pulled towards the Earth by gravity); gravity pulling the bungee jumper towards the Earth and the elastic rope pulling her up again; the weight of the boy (caused by gravity) squashes the springs and the springs push him up again; the girl pulls the elastic of the catapult and the elastic pushes the stone, making it move; the boy's weight pushes downwards (pulled by gravity) and squashes the spacehopper, and the spacehopper pushes him back up again; the boy's weight (caused by gravity) squashes the spring of the pogo stick and the spring pushes him up again.

> **Vocabulary:** *cause, force, gravity, push, pull, squash, weight.*

ICT **Floating forces** and **Check it** (pages 45–46) help the children to learn that more than one force may act on one object and that when an object is submerged in water, the water pushes it upwards. They are required to make careful measurements, to use a forcemeter accurately, to repeat, check and evaluate their measurements and to present their results in a table. This reinforces numeracy skills: measurement (weight) and data handling. By focusing on discrepancies the children are given an incentive to measure accurately and to read the scale on the forcemeter carefully. They are also encouraged to notice any differences in readings of different forcemeters. On page 46, ask the children to draw a bar in colour to represent the weight of the object each time they weigh it. They should each use a different colour and should number each record 1, 2 and 3. They could write their names under their section of the graph:

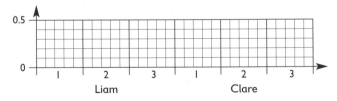

Once they have plotted their results on the graph, ask them if they think any group of results looks reliable and why, and which looks unreliable. A complementary activity for these sheets is available on the website (see Year 6 Activity 4).

Resources: bucket of water • forcemeters with different scales • objects to weigh: ball, book, brick, pencil case, shoe, stone, tin of food • plastic bags

> **Vocabulary:** *downwards, force, gravity, upthrust, upwards.*

It's elastic (page 47) develops the children's understanding that how much an elastic band stretches depends on the force acting on it. They should notice that the heavier the weight, the longer the elastic band (the more it stretches).

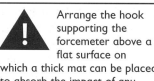 Arrange the hook supporting the forcemeter above a flat surface on which a thick mat can be placed to absorb the impact of any weights that might be dropped. Encourage the children to work carefully and to avoid dropping the weights.

Resources: forcemeters • elastic bands • yogurt pots • paper clips • rulers • weights

Vocabulary: *force, forcemeter, gravity, heavier, heavy, pull.*

Air force (page 48) develops the children's understanding of forces that act against one another by investigating the effects of air resistance on falling

 The children should not climb onto furniture to drop the papers.

objects. It is useful to reinforce the idea that objects do not 'just move'; they move if a force acts on them and if that force is greater than any forces acting against it. The pieces of paper fall to the ground because gravity pulls them, but the larger their surface area the more air is beneath them and the greater the air resistance, which acts against gravity.

Resources: A4 paper

Vocabulary: *air resistance, direction, downwards, force, gravity, upwards.*

How we see things

The activities in this section build on **Light and shadows** from **Year 3** and **Earth, Sun and Moon** from **Year 5**.

Beam blocker (page 49) develops the children's understanding that light travels from a source. It encourages them to use their knowledge

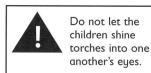 Do not let the children shine torches into one another's eyes.

about light to explain observations. You could provide an activity corner in which the children can explore light and shadows, make shadow puppets and so on. They should realise that a shadow is an area where there is no light because the light coming from a source is blocked. The children could make silhouettes by drawing around one another's shadows (cast by an overhead projector onto a piece of black paper fixed to a wall or display board), cutting around the outlines and mounting them on white paper. They could make ornate 'gilt' frames from painted cardboard for their silhouettes.

Resources: card • powerful torches • scissors

Vocabulary: *absorb, beam, block, light, opaque, ray, reflect, shadow, source.*

Now you see it (page 50) develops the children's learning about how we see light from sources (it enters our eyes) and how we see other objects (because light from a source is reflected from them into our eyes). You could show the children a darkened box with a small dark object in it (for example, a Plasticine figure).

Inside it, fix small light sources (such as bulbs powered by low-voltage batteries). Change the batteries to a higher voltage and discuss the effect (we can see things better if they are brighter).

Vocabulary: *beam, block, light, opaque, ray, reflect, shadow, source.*

Target practice (page 51) consolidates the children's learning about reflected light. They can use a mirror to reflect the light in the

 Warn the children not to shine torches into one another's eyes. Use plastic or metal mirrors.

direction they choose. Point out the angle at which they have to hold the mirror to make the light reflect onto the target. Move the position of the target and ask them what they should do with the mirror. In the extension activity the children can fix a mirror to the centre of the target so that it reflects light towards another target.

Resources: plane mirrors • scissors • torches

Vocabulary: *angle, beam, light, ray, reflect, source.*

In **Beam tracer** (page 52) the children learn that light from an object can be reflected by a mirror and that when a beam of

 Warn the children not to shine torches into one another's eyes. Use plastic or metal mirrors.

light is reflected from a surface, its direction changes. They learn the conventional symbol for a ray of light: a line with an arrowhead. They are encouraged to make careful observations and comparisons. Simple, battery-powered light boxes are available from educational suppliers such as Hope Education (www.hope-education.co.uk).

Resources: light box with a slit, or bright torch and a piece of card with a slit cut in it • plane mirrors • bulldog clips

Vocabulary: *angle, beam, light, light box ray, plane mirror, reflect, source.*

Enlarge it (page 53) helps the children to identify factors affecting the size of a shadow of an object and to investigate how changing one factor causes a shadow to change. Ask them why they think the shadow increases in size when they hold the smaller butterfly close to the light source (because it blocks out more light). Some children might be able to work out the relationships between distance from the light source and size of shadow. They could also try moving the position of one or other of the butterflies. This activity requires the children to use their mathematical skills in problem solving.

Resources: card • scissors • torches • long pins • corks • bulldog clips

Vocabulary: *enlarge, factor, light, reflect, reflection, source.*

Shadows and reflections (page 54) reviews the children's learning about shadows and reflections. Invite them to compare their sorting of the cards with that of another group. Discuss any differences and, if necessary, repeat some of the activities or provide similar ones in different contexts to ensure that the children understand that a shadow is formed when a beam of light is blocked by an opaque material and that reflection occurs when a light beam changes direction on hitting a shiny surface.

Resources: scissors

Vocabulary: *beam, direction, mirror, opaque, ray, reflection, shadow, shiny, source.*

Changing circuits

The activities in this section build on **Using electricity** from **Year 2** and **Circuits and conductors** from **Year 4**.

Who's there? (page 55) revises the children's previous learning about electrical circuits. As well as knowing that they should use a strong enough battery to make the buzzer or bell work, they should be aware of the dangers of using too strong a battery. You could demonstrate the danger of overloading a circuit by showing the children a circuit in which the battery is too powerful for the bulb (the bulb soon burns out).

Resources: buzzer or bell • batteries • battery-holders • wire • crocodile clips or battery snaps • switches • screwdrivers

Vocabulary: *battery, battery-holder, battery snaps, bell, buzzer, circuit, crocodile clip, overload, switch, wire.*

Circuit diagrams (page 56) explores the conventional symbols for components in circuits used in circuit diagrams. The children could draw a diagram for the circuit they made for a doorbell (see page 55). The symbols for a bell or a buzzer are:

 Remind the children that circuits made with batteries are safe, even if they touch the bare wires. Warn them of the dangers of mains electricity.

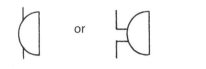

or

Vocabulary: *battery, bell, buzzer, circuit, diagram, wire.*

ICT In **Wired up** (page 57) the children learn that the brightness of bulbs in a circuit can be changed by changing the wiring and that circuit diagrams, using symbols, can be used for interpreting circuits. They could wire the bulbs in series:

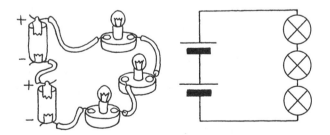

Give them the opportunity to find another way in which to wire the bulbs, so that they do not go dimmer each time a bulb is added (a parallel circuit):

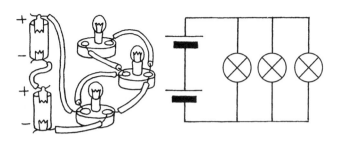

In the extension activity, the children will need to include two switches in parallel as follows:

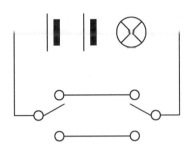

A complementary activity for this sheet is available on the website (see Year 6 Activity 5).

Resources: bulbs • bulb-holders • batteries • wire • crocodile clips or battery snaps • switches • screwdrivers

Vocabulary: *battery, bell, brightness, circuit, diagram, parallel, series, switch, volt, voltage, wire.*

Wire wise (page 58) helps the children to learn that the brightness of bulbs in a circuit can be changed by changing the wires. They are asked to suggest an investigation, select equipment, make fair comparisons and draw conclusions from these comparisons. Ask the children to read the voltages on batteries and to compare them with the voltage of mains electricity (220–240 volts). Point out that a higher voltage requires stronger wire, so that the wire will not burn out. You could take the opportunity to revise comparative and superlative adjectives and the ways in which the suffixes *-er* and *-est* affect their spellings (for example, doubling the final letter): *brighter, brightest, dimmer, dimmest.*

 Warn the children never to experiment with mains electricity.

Resources: bulbs • bulb-holders • batteries • crocodile clips or battery snaps • screwdrivers • strips of thin paper • different types of wire: fuse wire (5 amp, 15 amp and 30 amp), thin, single-strand bare wire (from educational suppliers), thin steel cotton-covered wire (also from educational suppliers, and useful for making electro-magnets), plastic-coated wire of different thicknesses (including the wire used for the flexes of electrical appliances), heavy-duty wire as used in mains wiring

Vocabulary: *battery, brightness, bulb, circuit, resistance, thickness, volt, voltage, wire.*

In **Dim it** (page 59) the children learn about a variable resistor (graphite – the 'lead' in a pencil); the activity also encourages them to explain their observations in terms of knowledge about electrical circuits. The children

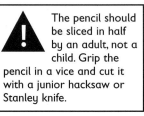

The pencil should be sliced in half by an adult, not a child. Grip the pencil in a vice and cut it with a junior hacksaw or Stanley knife.

should be able to use their knowledge of conductors and resistors and their recent learning about the effects of different wires in a circuit to help them to investigate the effects of varying the length of the pencil lead between the wires. You could also give them an opportunity to investigate the effect of using wires of very different lengths in a circuit. The longer the wire, the more resistance there is in the circuit, and the dimmer the bulb, but this might not be evident if the differences between the lengths of the wires are not great. A piece of graphite offers greater resistance than a piece of wire (which is usually made of copper) and so quite small differences in the length of the graphite have obvious effects on the brightness of the bulb.

Resources: bulbs • bulb-holders • batteries • wire • crocodile clips or battery snaps • screwdrivers • strips of thin paper • pencils sliced in half lengthways

Vocabulary: *battery, brightness, bulb, circuit, conductor, dimmer, graphite, length, resistance, resistor, variable, vary, volt, voltage, wire.*

Enquiry in environmental and technological contexts

The activities in this section focus on investigation. The children are encouraged to plan how to approach a problem, collect and record evidence appropriately, explain their results using scientific knowledge and understanding and evaluate the evidence collected and consider its limitations. It relates to the children's work in **Changing circuits** (see above).

Tilt switch (page 60) helps the children to use scientific knowledge to identify significant features of an artefact to be

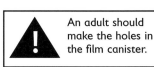

An adult should make the holes in the film canister.

designed. They are asked to follow instructions on how to make a tilt switch and then to test the switch. If the switch does not work, encourage the children to look for unwanted breaking or joining of the circuit: for example, metal parts in contact when they should not be and Blu-tack or sellotape covering metal parts that should be in contact.

Resources: 35mm film canisters with holes pierced in the lid and base • metal foil • wire • batteries • bulbs in holders • battery snaps • battery-holders • scissors • large ball-bearings that will fit inside film canisters • sticky tape • Blu-tack

Vocabulary: *ball-bearing, break, canister, circuit, connect, diagram, join, switch, tilt.*

Alarm (page 61) encourages the children to use scientific knowledge to identify significant features of an artefact to be designed, to plan a suitable approach to a design and to test their designs using their scientific knowledge and understanding. A tilt switch would be suitable for this. The children could use a manufactured tilt switch connected to computer software.

Resources: 35mm film canisters with holes pierced in the lid and base • metal foil • wire • batteries • bulbs in holders • battery snaps • battery-holders • scissors • large ball-bearings that will fit inside film canisters • sticky tape • Blu-tack

Vocabulary: *ball-bearing, break, canister, circuit, connect, diagram, join, switch, tilt.*

Pressure pad (page 62) encourages the children to use scientific knowledge to identify significant features of an artefact to be designed and to plan a suitable approach to a design. A pressure pad switch can be made in several ways, including the following:

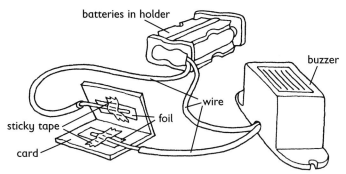

Resources: batteries and holder • wire • buzzer or bell • card • foam • sticky tape • glue • metal foil

Vocabulary: *contact, join, pressure pad, switch.*

In **Switch test** (page 63) the children are asked to test designs, using scientific knowledge and understanding. It is an opportunity for the children to use circuit diagrams in a meaningful context. Encourage the children not to scrap completely a switch that does not work, but to examine one component at a time.

Resources: batteries and holder • wire • buzzer or bell • card • foam • sticky tape • glue • metal foil

Vocabulary: *break, circuit, component, contact, join, switch.*

In **Trial log** (page 64) the children are asked to test something they have designed and made, making a series of observations. They are asked to adjust their designs in a systematic way in the light of the evidence they collect. It helps them to evaluate the limitations of their designs and those of others and to keep a record of the alterations they have made. It could be used in conjunction with work in design and technology.

Vocabulary: *component, evaluate, evaluation, evidence, improve.*

Dark to light

Understand that green plants need light

- **Observe a plant that has been kept in the dark for a week or two.**

- **Predict how it will change if you keep it in the light for a week.**

	Dark (observations) 🌙	Light (predictions) ☀
Stem Note: – colour – length – strength.		
Leaves Note: – colour – strength – how many – size.		

Now try this!

- **Explain why the plant will change in the ways you have predicted.**

- **Find out if you are right by observing the same plant in the light.**

- **Use information sources to find out how plants use light.**

Teachers' note Remind the children of their previous learning about the needs of plants. What do they remember about plants that were kept in the dark? You could also draw their attention to the ways in which plants grow towards a light source.

Developing Science
Year 6
© A & C Black

Plant key: plants

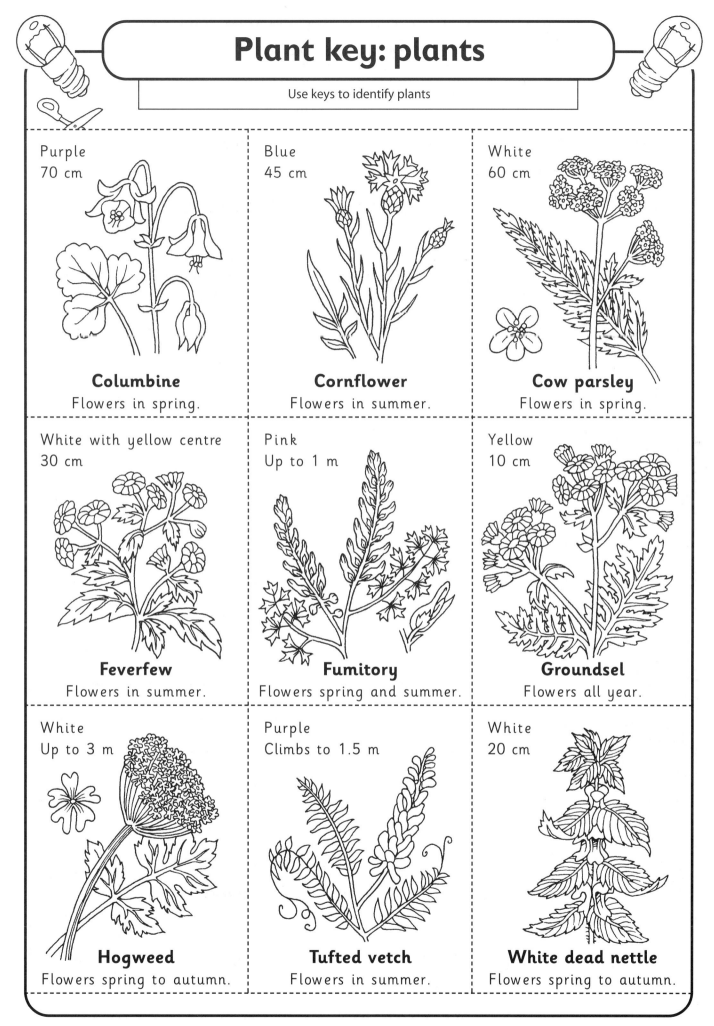

Purple
70 cm

Columbine

Flowers in spring.

Blue
45 cm

Cornflower

Flowers in summer.

White
60 cm

Cow parsley

Flowers in spring.

White with yellow centre
30 cm

Feverfew

Flowers in summer.

Pink
Up to 1 m

Fumitory

Flowers spring and summer.

Yellow
10 cm

Groundsel

Flowers all year.

White
Up to 3 m

Hogweed

Flowers spring to autumn.

Purple
Climbs to 1.5 m

Tufted vetch

Flowers in summer.

White
20 cm

White dead nettle

Flowers spring to autumn.

Teachers' note This page can be used in different ways. The children can use the pictures, along with the questions on page 16, to create a key to help others to recognise them, or lower-attaining children could learn to distinguish between plants by using the pictures to play a 'Guess who?' type game (see page 5).

**Developing Science
Year 6
© A & C Black**

Plant key: questions

Use keys to identify plants

Does it have blue flowers?	Does it have purple flowers?	Does it have pink flowers?	Does it have white flowers?
Does it have yellow flowers?	Does it have round, flat flowers?	Does it have bell-shaped flowers?	Does it have long flowers?
Does it have broad, flat leaves?	Does it have long, thin leaves?	Do the leaves grow in pairs?	Do the leaves have serrated edges?
Does it have tendrils?	Do the flowers grow in groups?	Do the flowers grow on umbels?	Does it have feathery leaves?

Teachers' note Use this with page 15 (see page 5). Remind the children of their previous use of questions to split a group of plants or animals into two sub-groups. They could also create a key for the plants or animals they have identified in a local habitat. Discuss the features that distinguish a plant (or animal) from others. Ensure the children understand all the vocabulary needed to complete the task (for example, *umbel*: a cluster of flowers growing on short stalks from a central point).

**Developing Science
Year 6
© A & C Black**

Pond food web

Understand that animals and plants in a habitat are interdependent

These are a few of the animals found around ponds.

The animals eat only the things below them on the food web.

heron

perch   frog

great diving beetle   stickleback

common newt

water flea   worm   tadpole

algae, pondweed and other plants

• **Write what the animals eat.**

perch

I eat _____

_____

_____

I eat perch,_____

_____

_____

heron

worm

I eat _____

_____

_____

I eat _____

_____

_____

common newt

I eat _____

_____

_____

great diving beetle

I eat _____

_____

_____

frog tadpole

Now try this!

• **What are at the bottom of the** food web **?**
• **Write a report about what food they need.**

Teachers' note Revise the children's previous learning about food chains. What happens at the bottom of a food chain? What does that living thing eat? Show them the food web and explain that it is similar to a food chain, but enables them to record more information. Discuss what happens at the bottom of the food web.

Developing Science
Year 6
© A & C Black

Your web

- ## Make notes about a |habitat|.

  ### What do the animals eat?

Habitat _____

Animal	What it eats	What eats it

- ## Use your notes to help you to make a |food web|.

Now try this!

- ## Identify an animal that helps the habitat.
- ## Write an explanation about how it helps.

Teachers' note The children should first have completed page 17. Use this page to help them to record what they have found out about the feeding relationships of animals and plants in a local habitat. The children could first find the animals at the top of the food web by reading through their notes to find those that nothing else in the habitat eats.

Developing Science
Year 6
© **A & C Black**

Soil match

Understand that different plants grow in different soil conditions

Do plants grow better in some types of soil than in others?

You could plant some seeds in:

| sandy soil | chalky soil | clay soil |

How will you make the test fair?

_____

_____

_____

_____

Think about water, light and warmth.

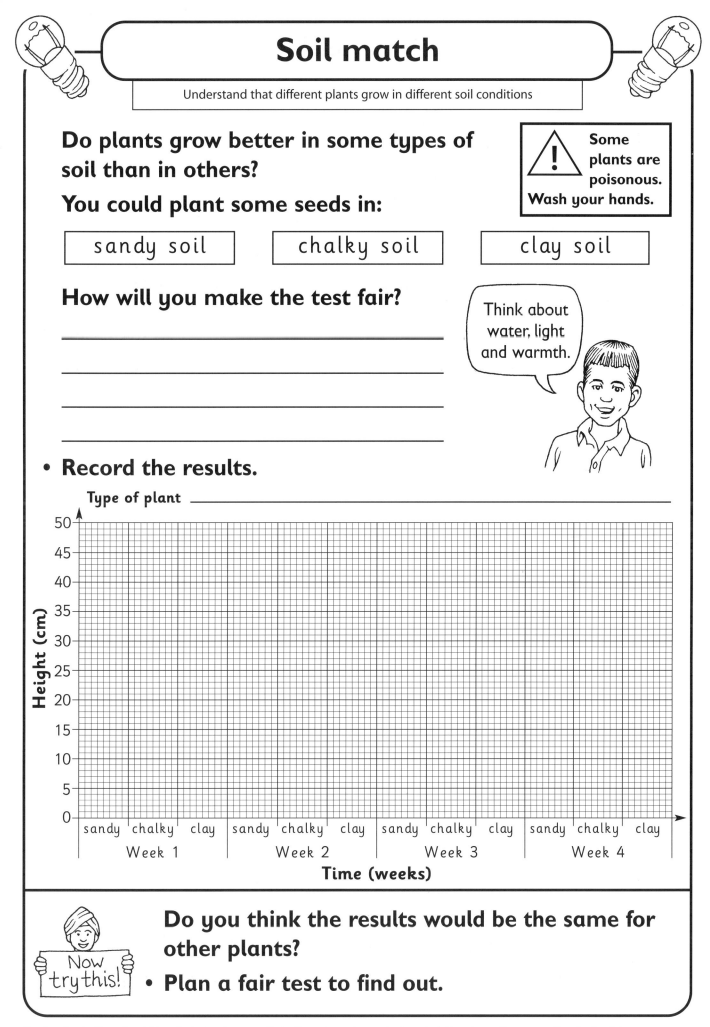

• **Record the results.**

Type of plant _____

Height (cm) / Time (weeks)

sandy chalky clay — Week 1
sandy chalky clay — Week 2
sandy chalky clay — Week 3
sandy chalky clay — Week 4

Now try this!

Do you think the results would be the same for other plants?

• **Plan a fair test to find out.**

Teachers' note Show the children the instructions supplied with garden or house plants and ask them to use these to answer the question *Does the type of soil make any difference to the growth of plants?* Let the children examine samples of different types of soil using hand lenses. Ask them to notice the differences in colour and size of particles.

Developing Science
Year 6
© A & C Black

19

Fertilisers

Recognise that fertilisers are used to provide plants with nutrients

What difference do you think a fertiliser **will make to a plant?**

_____

_____

⚠ Wash your hands after handling soil, fertilisers and plants.

- **Plan a fair test to check your prediction.**

Use plants, not seeds.

This is what I shall do:	I shall need:
I shall keep these things the same:	I shall change only this:

What I shall observe or measure:

If my prediction is right, this is what I expect to happen:

Now try this!

Which is the best fertiliser?

Will this be the same for different plants?

- **Make notes about how you can find out.**

Teachers' note The children should first have completed page 19. Ask them if they know how garden soil can be improved to help plants to grow well. Show them some proprietary plant foods and ask them if they know why people add these to the water they give to plants. Remind them that plants produce their own food from gases in the air and add that some minerals are taken in with water through the roots.

Developing Science Year 6
© A & C Black

The seashore

Understand that different animals and plants are found in different habitats

What makes the seashore a good habitat for these animals?

Find out what the animals eat, and how they live and breed.

Herring gull

Sand eel

Shore crab

Barnacle

Sea anemone

Sand smelt

- **Choose an animal that you have observed in its habitat.**
- **Make notes and write a report about why the animal is suited to this habitat.**

Now try this!

Teachers' note This page could be used in conjunction with a visit to a beach or with secondary sources such as videos, posters and books. Encourage the children to use the primary or secondary sources to answer the question *What makes the seashore a good place for this animal to live, feed or breed?*

Developing Science
Year 6
© A & C Black

Habitat watch

ICT

Understand how animals and plants are suited to their environment

- **Use this page to record the plants and animals in a** habitat **, and what makes the habitat suitable for them.**

⚠️ Treat plants and animals with care. Try not to disturb habitats.

Use information books.

Habitat description:

Plant or animal	What makes the habitat suitable for it

Now try this!

- **Study one plant or animal in detail.**
- **List the places where you have seen it.**
- **Describe the habitats and say why they are suitable.**

Teachers' note It would be helpful if the children had first completed page 21. They can use this page to record their observations of animals or plants in a habitat they have studied: for example, walls, hedges, paths, flowerbeds, fallen trees. They could work in groups, with each member researching a different animal or plant. Set them the task of considering why each animal or plant is found in that habitat. What conditions make the habitat suitable?

Developing Science
Year 6
© **A & C Black**

A question of illness

- **Think of a time when you were ill.**

  What was wrong with you? _____

  _____

  What might have caused it?

  _____   Write in note form.

- **Fill in the chart to help you find out more about the illness.**

This is what I know	My questions	Where I can find the answers	Answers

- **Choose one of your questions.**
- **Write a report to answer it.**

Now try this!

Use books, CD-ROMs and the Internet.

Teachers' note Ask the children to name anything they can think of that can make people ill. They might know the terms *germ* and *virus*. Explain that *germ* is an everyday term for a *micro-organism*. Some micro-organisms can make people ill. Discuss how these micro-organisms can get into the body (through openings such as cuts, the mouth, the nose and around the eyes). The children should use information books, CD-ROMs and videos to find the answers to their questions.

Developing Science
Year 6
© **A & C Black**

23

Mouldy matters

Understand that micro-organisms can cause food to decay

- **Observe some** mould .
- **Draw and write about your observations.**

Use colours.

Where is the mould?	
Description	
Colours	
Shapes and patterns	Labelled drawing
Anything else you notice	

Now try this!

What do you think made the mould grow?

_____

_____

What is mould? _____

_____

_____

_____

Write a definition.

How would you stop food going mouldy?

_____

_____

Teachers' note Show the children some (covered and sealed) mouldy food such as fruit, cheese or bread and ask them to describe what has happened to the food. Keep the food in a place where it cannot be handled by the children and let them look at it at intervals over the course of a week or two. Point out that the mould itself is not a living organism but is the changed food. (The change is caused by the micro-organisms living on the food.)

**Developing Science
Year 6**
© A & C Black

Barbecue bugs

Recognise that food needs to be handled and stored with care

- **Explain why people should follow these rules if they have a barbecue.**

Write on the chart.

At your barbecue

1 Wash your hands before handling food.
2 Wash your hands after handling raw meat.
3 Keep all food covered until needed.
4 Keep cold food refrigerated until needed.
5 Use separate utensils and containers for raw meat and other foods.
6 Do not reheat food.
7 Ensure that meat and foods containing meat (such as sausages and burgers) are cooked thoroughly.

Rule	Reason
1	
2	
3	
4	
5	
6	
7	

- **Write a report about the food hygiene rules followed by your school kitchen or a local restaurant or food shop.**

Teachers' note Ask the children what food hygiene rules they know. Write up their responses and discuss why these rules are important. What might happen if they were not followed? Revise or explain that micro-organisms (germs) can enter the body on food and can cause food poisoning. Ask the children to discuss the rules on this page with their groups. Invite feedback and ask the children to check their responses in information books.

Developing Science
Year 6
© A & C Black

A lot of rot

Find out how materials change:

wire tie
(leave space
to let air in
and out)

clear plastic bag

grass cuttings
or fallen leaves

You need

a clear plastic bag

a wire tie

grass cuttings
or leaves

⚠ **Do not open
the bag.**

- **Observe the material for two weeks.**
- **Record any changes.**

Material:

Feel the
outside of
the bag.

Date	Look	Smell (not too close)	Feel

Now try this!

- **Write about ways in which the action of decay can be beneficial.**

Teachers' note Ask the children to predict what will happen to the leaves or grass cuttings and to explain their predictions. Help them to make links between their ideas and what they know about rotting food (page 24). What do they think is causing the changes? Remind them about their previous learning about micro-organisms. For the practical activity, the plastic bag prevents the materials from drying out.

Developing Science
Year 6
© **A & C Black**

A vital ingredient

Understand that micro-organisms feed and grow

Why is `yeast` **used in bread-making?**

_____

_____

Find out more about yeast:

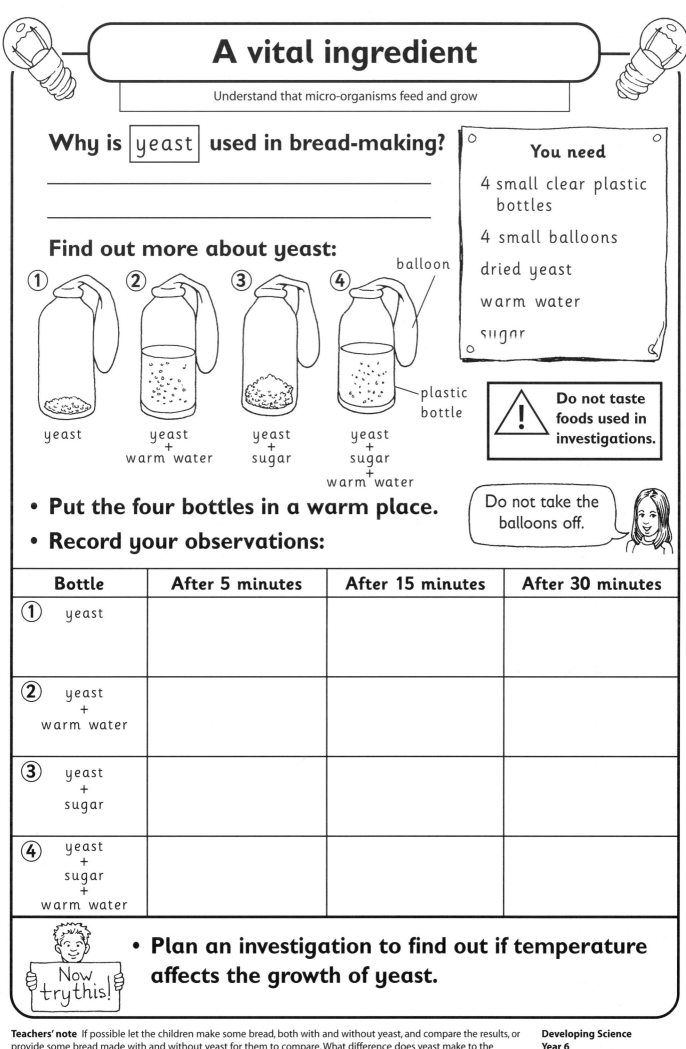

balloon

① yeast

② yeast + warm water

③ yeast + sugar

④ yeast + sugar + warm water

plastic bottle

You need

4 small clear plastic bottles

4 small balloons

dried yeast

warm water

sugar

⚠ **Do not taste foods used in investigations.**

- **Put the four bottles in a warm place.**

Do not take the balloons off.

- **Record your observations:**

Bottle	After 5 minutes	After 15 minutes	After 30 minutes
① yeast			
② yeast + warm water			
③ yeast + sugar			
④ yeast + sugar + warm water			

Now try this!

- **Plan an investigation to find out if temperature affects the growth of yeast.**

Teachers' note If possible let the children make some bread, both with and without yeast, and compare the results, or provide some bread made with and without yeast for them to compare. What difference does yeast make to the appearance, texture and feel of bread? Point out the holes in the dough and discuss what made them (see page 7). In the activity use about half a teaspoonful of dried yeast and a teaspoonful of sugar.

Developing Science
Year 6
© **A & C Black**

Yummy yogurt

Recognise that micro-organisms are useful in food production

- **Read the ingredients of a pot of natural yogurt and a pot of natural 'live' yogurt.**
  Natural Yogurt Natural Live Yogurt

  What difference do you notice?

  _____

  _____

  _____

  _____

- **Make some yogurt.**

  ⚠ **Wash your hands. Keep everything clean.**

You need

a pot of natural yogurt

a pot of natural 'live' yogurt

300 ml cold milk

300 ml hot milk

wide-necked flask or insulated jar

tablespoon

basin

measuring jug

whisk

fridge

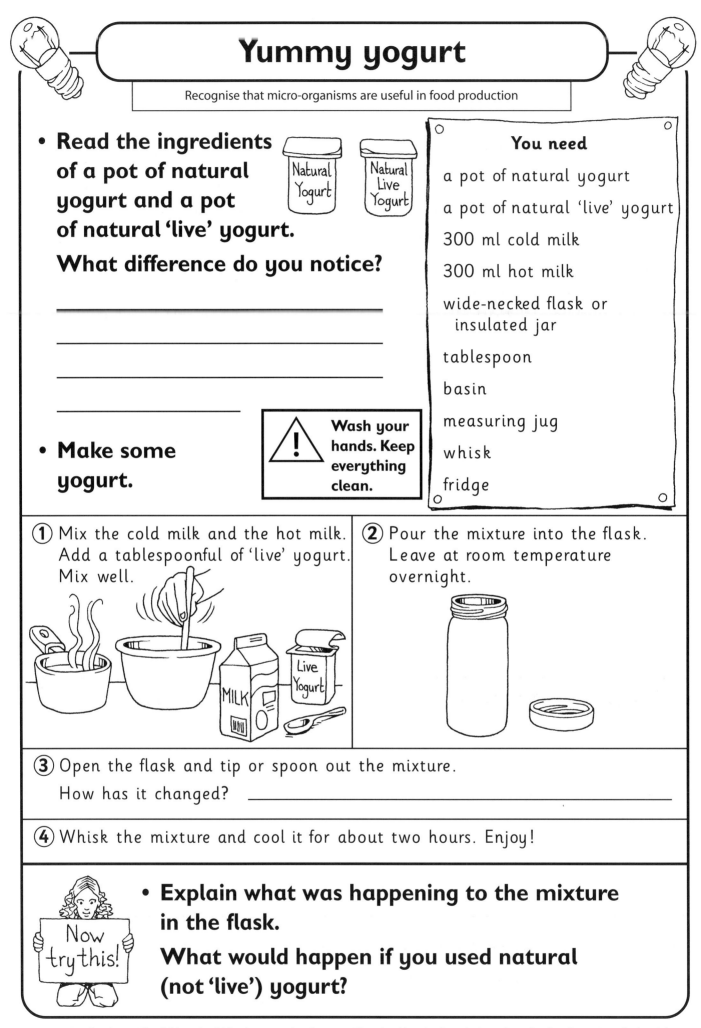

① Mix the cold milk and the hot milk. Add a tablespoonful of 'live' yogurt. Mix well.

② Pour the mixture into the flask. Leave at room temperature overnight.

③ Open the flask and tip or spoon out the mixture. How has it changed? _____

④ Whisk the mixture and cool it for about two hours. Enjoy!

Now try this!

- **Explain what was happening to the mixture in the flask.**

- **What would happen if you used natural (not 'live') yogurt?**

Teachers' note The children should first have completed page 27. They should notice from the ingredients list that the live yogurt contains a living organism (a bacterium named lactobacillus), but that ordinary natural yogurt does not. You could link this with their previous learning about the action of yeast on bread dough (noting that this stops at high temperatures and does not re-start).

Developing Science
Year 6
© **A & C Black**

Clean up

Understand that insoluble solids can be separated from water by filtering

How can you get the dirt out of water from a puddle?

⚠ **Wash your hands afterwards. Do not drink the water.**

- **Use this page to help you to plan, record your results and evaluate.**

This is what I shall do:

I shall need:

My idea will work because…

This is what happened:

It happened because…

Evaluation:

Now try this!

- **Write instructions to help someone else to clean up some dirty water.**

Teachers' note Show the children some water containing mud and gravel and ask them to describe it. Can they think of a way of removing the mud and gravel from the water? Ask them why they think their ideas will work. After discussing their plans (written on this page) and modifying them if necessary, let them try out their ideas. They should keep some of the original water to compare with their 'cleaned' water. Is it pure, or does it just look cleaner?

Developing Science
Year 6
© **A & C Black**

What's in it?

Recognise that when solids dissolve in water a clear solution is formed

Which liquids contain dissolved materials?

Hint: How can you separate dissolved materials from water?

- **Predict, and then think of a way to find out.**

Liquid	What might be dissolved in the water?	How I can find out	Results
filtered water			
sea water			
tap water			
ink			
distilled water			
tea			

Now try this!

- **List some other** solutions **you know.**
- **Find out what is dissolved in the solutions.**
- **Write whether it is dissolved in water in each case.**

Teachers' note Remind the children about what they separated from the water on page 29. Had the mud and gravel dissolved? How do they know? Show them the liquids listed on the chart and ask them which ones contain dissolved materials. Can dissolved materials be separated from water by sieving or filtering? (Remind them of everyday filters such as teabags, which allow dissolved materials to pass through but not the undissolved tea leaves.)

Developing Science
Year 6
© **A & C Black**

Steamy stuff

Make and test predictions about water containing dissolved materials

- **Write what each solution is like.**
- **Predict what the** condensed water **will be like when the solution is heated.**

> ⚠ An adult must heat the liquid and hold the plate.
> Everything must be clean so that you can taste the solutions and the condensed water. Do not taste the ink.

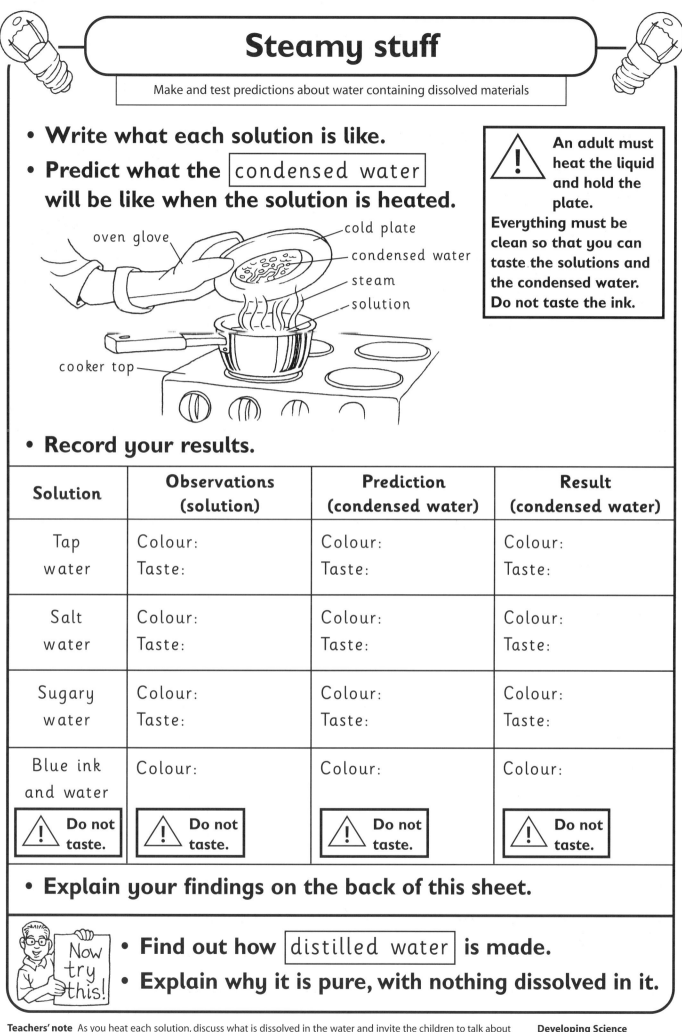

oven glove
cold plate
condensed water
steam
solution
cooker top

- **Record your results.**

Solution	Observations (solution)	Prediction (condensed water)	Result (condensed water)
Tap water	Colour: Taste:	Colour: Taste:	Colour: Taste:
Salt water	Colour: Taste:	Colour: Taste:	Colour: Taste:
Sugary water	Colour: Taste:	Colour: Taste:	Colour: Taste:
Blue ink and water ⚠ Do not taste.	Colour: ⚠ Do not taste.	Colour: ⚠ Do not taste.	Colour: ⚠ Do not taste.

- **Explain your findings on the back of this sheet.**

Now try this!
- **Find out how** distilled water **is made.**
- **Explain why it is pure, with nothing dissolved in it.**

Teachers' note As you heat each solution, discuss what is dissolved in the water and invite the children to talk about what is happening to the water and the material dissolved in it. Remind them about their previous learning about reversible changes and about boiling point.

Developing Science
Year 6
© A & C Black

'Frosted' glass

Understand that when liquid evaporates from a solution the solid remains

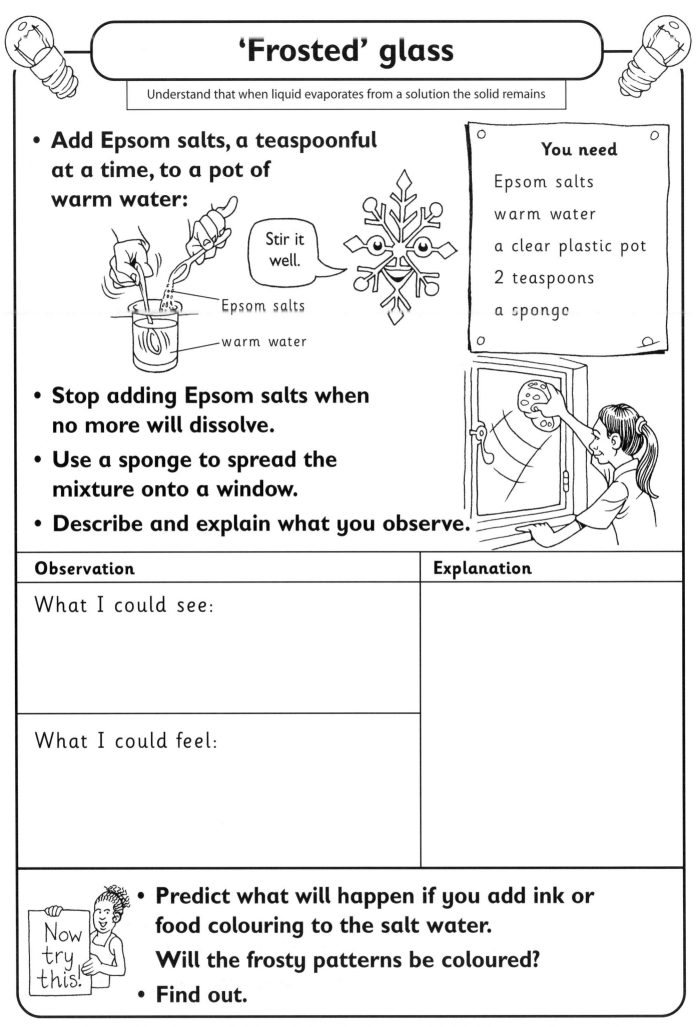

- **Add Epsom salts, a teaspoonful at a time, to a pot of warm water:**

Stir it well.

Epsom salts

warm water

You need

Epsom salts

warm water

a clear plastic pot

2 teaspoons

a sponge

- **Stop adding Epsom salts when no more will dissolve.**
- **Use a sponge to spread the mixture onto a window.**
- **Describe and explain what you observe.**

Observation	Explanation
What I could see:	
What I could feel:	

- **Predict what will happen if you add ink or food colouring to the salt water.**

  Will the frosty patterns be coloured?
- **Find out.**

Now try this!

Teachers' note Ask the children to notice if Epsom salts dissolve in water and to predict what will happen when the water evaporates. What will be left on the window?

Developing Science
Year 6
© A & C Black

Quick dissolvers

Which type of sugar will dissolve most quickly?

- **Predict, and put the sugars in order.**

You need

caster sugar	sugar cubes
demerara sugar	2 teaspoons
granulated sugar	5 clear plastic pots
icing sugar	water

slowest dissolving ⟶ fastest dissolving

How can you test your predictions?

The test:	Making it fair:
How I can tell if the sugar has dissolved:	**What I shall observe, measure and record:**

- **Swap your work with a friend.**
- **Suggest two things your friend could do next time to improve the investigation.**

Now try this!

Teachers' note Ask the children to look at and feel the different sugars and to talk about their observations: for example, the colour of the sugar, the size of the particles and so on. When they predict the order in which they will dissolve they should give reasons. If the children time how long each sugar takes to dissolve they could record their findings on page 34; if they count the number of stirs they could use the graph on page 36.

Developing Science
Year 6
© **A & C Black**

Dissolving time

Understand that repeated measurements provide more reliable data

You need

caster sugar
demerara sugar
granulated sugar
icing sugar
sugar cubes
2 teaspoons
5 clear plastic pots
warm water
a timer

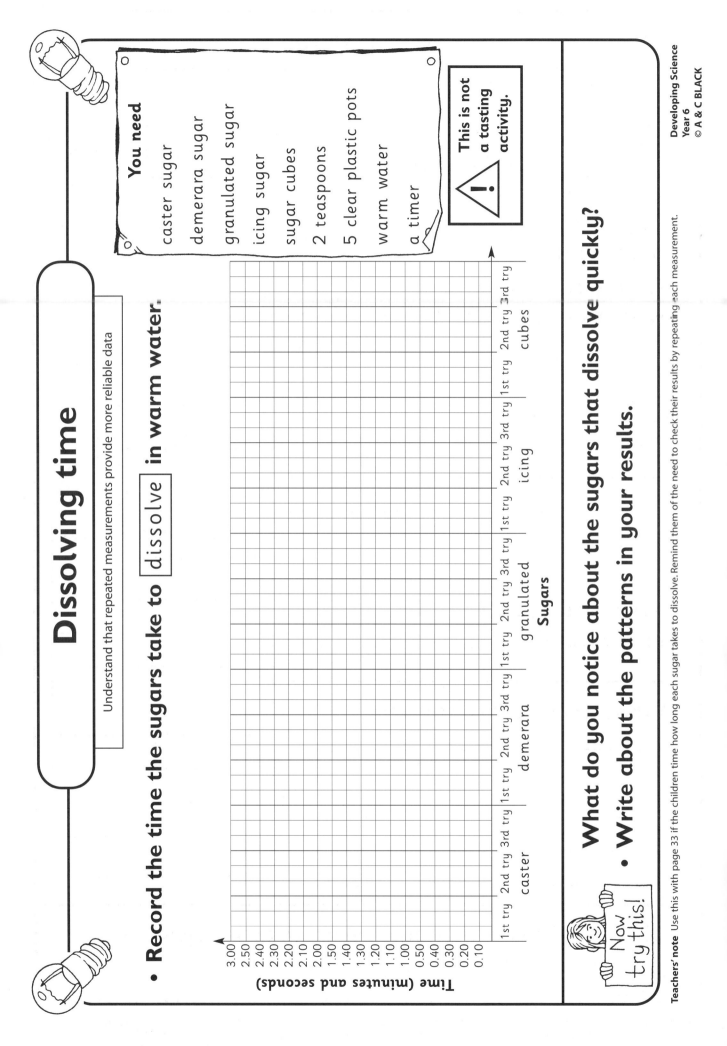

⚠️ **This is not a tasting activity.**

- ## Record the time the sugars take to | dissolve | in warm water.

Time (minutes and seconds)

3.00
2.50
2.40
2.30
2.20
2.10
2.00
1.50
1.40
1.30
1.20
1.10
1.00
0.50
0.40
0.30
0.20
0.10

| 1st try 2nd try 3rd try | 1st try 2nd try 3rd try | 1st try 2nd try 3rd try | 1st try 2nd try 3rd try | 1st try 2nd try 3rd try |
| caster | demerara | granulated | icing | cubes |

Sugars

- ## What do you notice about the sugars that dissolve quickly?
- ## Write about the patterns in your results.

Now try this!

Teachers' note Use this with page 33 if the children time how long each sugar takes to dissolve. Remind them of the need to check their results by repeating each measurement.

Developing Science
Year 6
© A & C BLACK

Speed it up

How can you make sugar dissolve more quickly?

- **On the teacup, list the things that might make a difference.**

- **On the teaspoon below, write the one you will test:**

These might make a difference

_____

_____

_____

_____

_____

How will you test your idea?

_____

_____

_____

_____

How will you know if it made any difference?

What will you observe, count or measure? _____

_____

I shall know it made a difference if...

_____

_____

What will you keep the same?

_____

_____

_____

_____

_____

_____

_____

_____

_____

_____

Now try this!

- **Explain how you will check your results to make sure they are right.**

Teachers' note The children should first have completed pages 33–34. Ask them what they noticed about the speed at which the sugar dissolved; what can they do to make this quicker? Discuss what people usually do when they add sugar to tea or coffee and what happens if they do not stir drinks. The graph on page 36 can be used for recording their results. **Developing Science Year 6** © **A & C Black**

Graph it

Use a graph to present results

Count how many stirs are needed to dissolve the sugar.

You need

hot and cold water to mix

ice for cooling

clear plastic pots

teaspoons

sugar

a thermometer

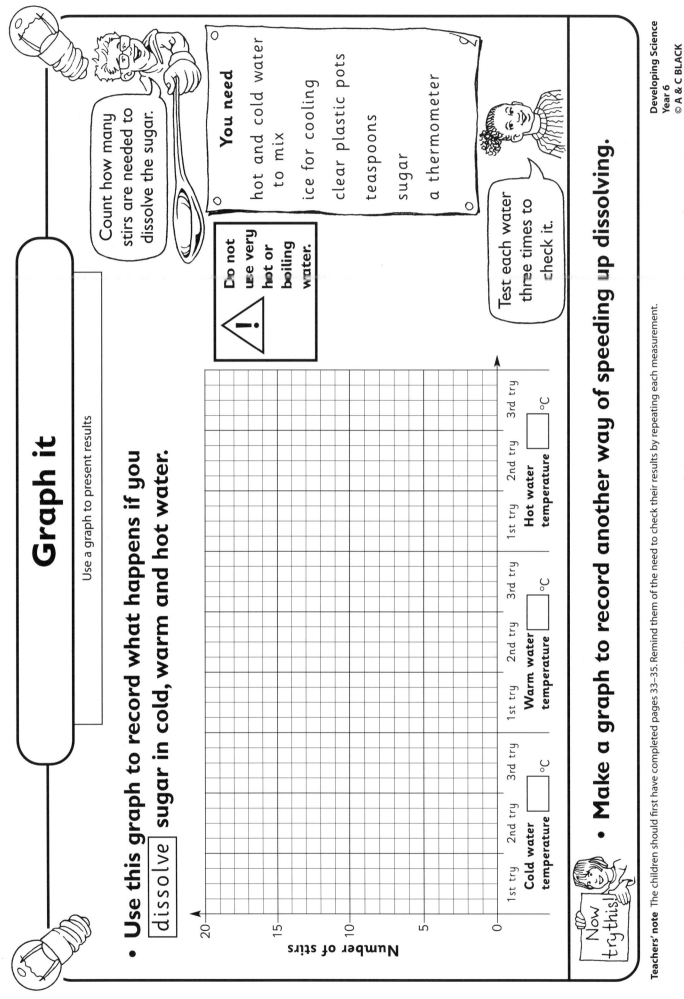

Do not use very hot or boiling water.

Test each water three times to check it.

- **Use this graph to record what happens if you dissolve sugar in cold, warm and hot water.**

Number of stirs

20

15

10

5

0

Cold water temperature ☐ °C
1st try | 2nd try | 3rd try

Warm water temperature ☐ °C
1st try | 2nd try | 3rd try

Hot water temperature ☐ °C
1st try | 2nd try | 3rd try

Now try this!

- **Make a graph to record another way of speeding up dissolving.**

Teachers' note The children should first have completed pages 33–35. Remind them of the need to check their results by repeating each measurement.

Developing Science
Year 6
© A & C BLACK

Mix it up

- **Mix each solid material with water.**
- **Watch what happens.**
- **List the materials in the correct groups below.**

⚠️ **Do not taste any of the mixtures.**

* An adult must make the cement mixture.

You need

clear plastic pots
plastic spoons
water
Andrews salts
baking powder
cement*
cornflour
Epsom salts
flour
plaster of Paris
powder paint
sand
tea leaves

Dissolved

Rinse the spoon and pot each time if you can. Keep one spoon dry.

Did not dissolve

A different type of change

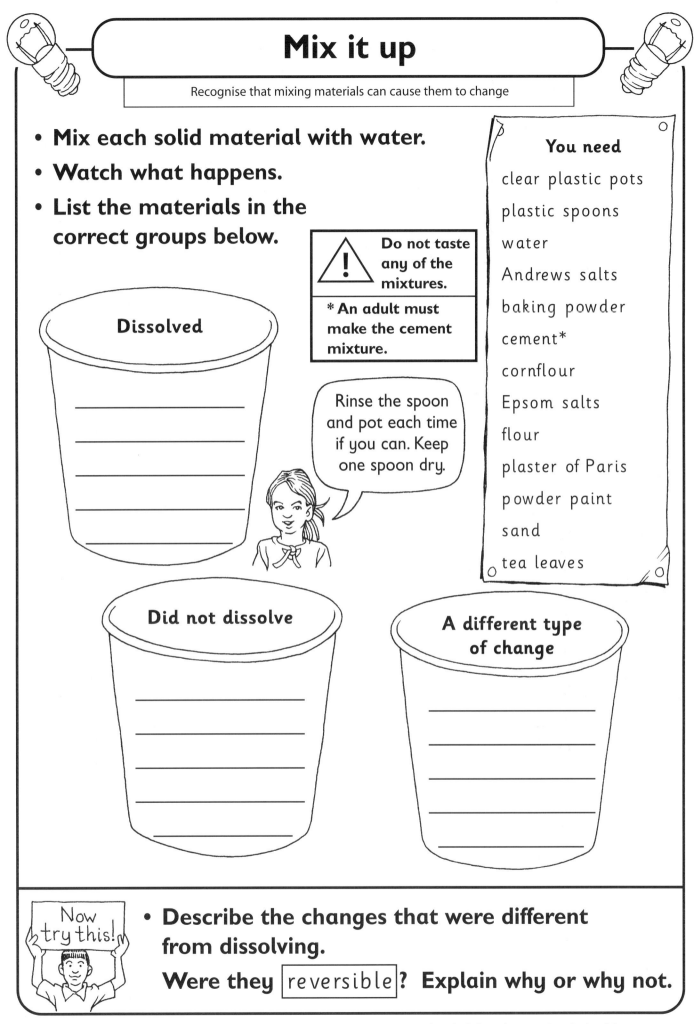

Now try this!

- **Describe the changes that were different from dissolving.**

  Were they | reversible |**? Explain why or why not.**

Teachers' note Revise the children's previous learning about dissolving and separating materials and ask them about other everyday mixtures of liquids and solids. What happens when they make these mixtures? Examples include making tea and coffee, and mixing cakes. Ask them if they know which materials dissolve and which do not, and how they know.

Developing Science
Year 6
© **A & C Black**

Time for a change

Make, record and explain careful observations

Which mixtures can be separated?

Mixture	Can it be separated?	If 'no', why not? If 'yes', how?
a sand + water		
b salt + water		
c plaster of Paris + water		
d flour + water		
e sugar + water		
f tea leaves + water		
g cement* + water	*An adult tests this.	
h Epsom salts + water		

List the mixtures that are reversible changes:

_____

Can you separate the mixtures below?

If not, why not? If you can, how?

| salt + sand + water | sugar + salt + water |

Teachers' note The children should first have completed page 37. Begin by asking them how they could separate a mixture of marbles and water, then a mixture of dried peas and water, then gravel and water; give other examples, gradually reducing the size of the particles so that the children realise that what is required is something with smaller and smaller holes. Point out that filter paper works in the same way as a sieve, but the holes are much smaller.

Developing Science
Year 6
© **A & C Black**

Sherbet fizz

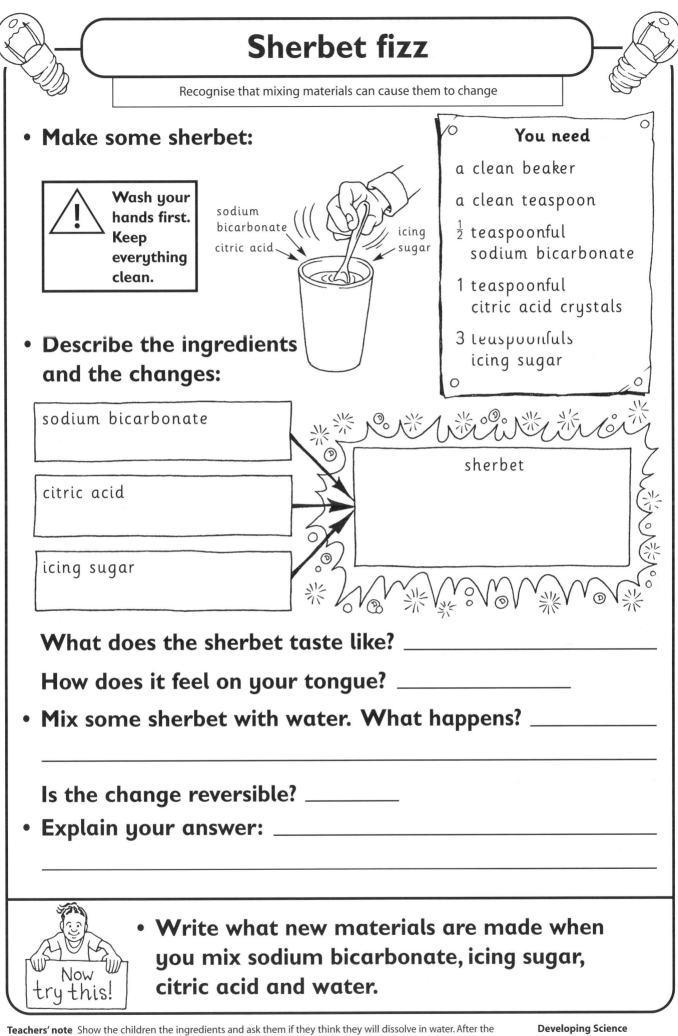

- **Make some sherbet:**

⚠ Wash your hands first. Keep everything clean.

sodium bicarbonate
citric acid
icing sugar

You need

a clean beaker

a clean teaspoon

$\frac{1}{2}$ teaspoonful sodium bicarbonate

1 teaspoonful citric acid crystals

3 teaspoonfuls icing sugar

- **Describe the ingredients and the changes:**

| sodium bicarbonate |
| citric acid |
| icing sugar |

sherbet

What does the sherbet taste like? _____

How does it feel on your tongue? _____

- **Mix some sherbet with water. What happens?** _____

_____

Is the change reversible? _____

- **Explain your answer:** _____

_____

Now try this!

- **Write what new materials are made when you mix sodium bicarbonate, icing sugar, citric acid and water.**

Teachers' note Show the children the ingredients and ask them if they think they will dissolve in water. After the children have made (and eaten!) the sherbet, ask them if they think any of the materials can be separated from the water and from one another. What clue shows that a new material has been made?

Developing Science
Year 6
© A & C Black

Hot and cold

Recognise that heating or cooling causes some materials to change

- **Describe the changes when each material is heated and cooled.
Are the changes** reversible **?**

Material	Heated		Cooled	
	Changes	Reversible? Explain.	Changes	Reversible? Explain.
ice				
water				
butter				
raw egg				
cake mixture				
unfired clay				
chocolate				

Now try this!

- **Collect four other examples of** reversible **changes and** irreversible **changes.**

Teachers' note Remind the children about their previous work on heating and cooling water. Ask them to describe the changes and to say whether or not they were reversible. The changes from ice to water to steam, and vice versa, are all reversible. Can the children think of any other heat changes that can be reversed?

Developing Science
Year 6
© A & C BLACK

Burn up

Recognise that when materials are burned, new materials are formed

- **Predict which materials will burn.**
- **Write on the chart.**
- **Test your predictions like this:**

tongs

material being tested

nightlight

sand

metal tray

pot of sand for putting out fires

You need

the equipment in the picture

a small twig

tiny pieces of different fabrics, polythene, metal, paper, foil, card, dry grass, newly-cut grass

⚠ **Do not lean over candles.
Tie back long hair.
Keep burning materials in the sand tray.
Don't breathe in the fumes.**

Prediction		Test		
Object or material	Will it burn?	Did it burn?	How did it change?	What new materials were formed?
twig				
cotton				
wool				
polyester				
polythene				
metal				
paper				
foil				
card				
dry grass				
new grass				

Now try this!

- **Were the changes** reversible **?**
- **Explain your answer.**

Teachers' note The teacher will probably have to demonstrate rather than allowing the pupils to burn materials. Your school or local authority guidelines might prohibit the use of naked flames, and so it will be necessary to show a video of material burning (you might have to change the chart according to what the children have observed). See pages 9–10 for other ideas if a practical activity is not possible.

**Developing Science
Year 6**
© A & C Black

41

Candlelight

Recognise that changes caused by burning are not reversible

- **Predict how a candle will change when it is burned and then cooled:** _____

_____

_____

_____

You need

candle

matches*

sand in foil dish

scales

ruler

Plasticine

Will the changes be boxed: reversible **?** _____

Will a new material be made? _____

- **Burn a candle like this:**

spare sand for putting out fires

⚠ *An adult must light the candle.
Tie back long hair.
Do not lean over flames.

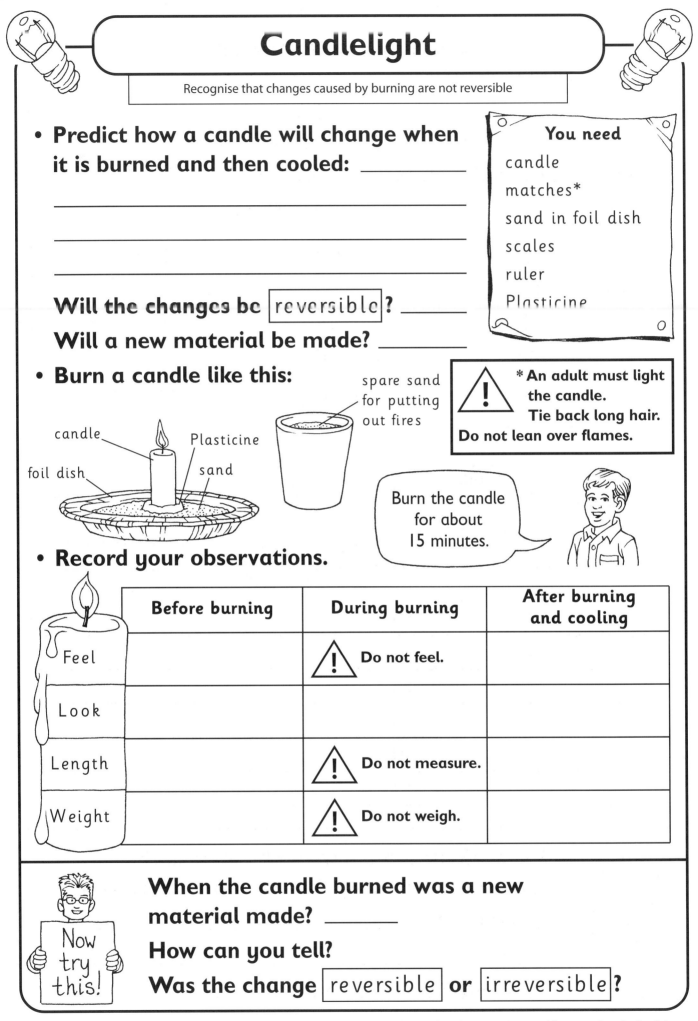

candle

Plasticine

foil dish

sand

Burn the candle for about 15 minutes.

- **Record your observations.**

	Before burning	During burning	After burning and cooling
Feel		⚠ **Do not feel.**	
Look			
Length		⚠ **Do not measure.**	
Weight		⚠ **Do not weigh.**	

Now try this!

When the candle burned was a new material made? _____

How can you tell?

Was the change reversible **or** irreversible **?**

Teachers' note The children should first have completed page 41. This might have to be a demonstration or a video (you could make a video of the demonstration if your school does not allow naked flames). Include pauses so that you can stop it easily to ask the children questions.

**Developing Science
Year 6**
© A & C Black

Measure the force

Understand that weight is a force measured in newtons

• Use a [forcemeter] to weigh some objects.

You could put each object into a plastic bag ...   ... or tie it with string.

forcemeter

plastic bag

string

object

What does the reading mean?

Object	Reading on forcemeter in newtons
	N
	N
	N
	N
	N
	N
	N
	N

_____
_____
_____
_____
_____
_____

Now try this!

What do you think would happen to the forcemeter readings for the same objects on:

the Moon? _____

Jupiter? _____

• **Find out from information books.**

Teachers' note Revise the use of forcemeters and ensure that the children know how to read the scale. Discuss what happens to the spring on the forcemeter when an object is hung from it. What pulls the object downwards? Why do some objects pull the spring more than others?

**Developing Science
Year 6**
© A & C Black

All kinds of forces

Recognise that several forces may act on one object

What forces can you find in the pictures?
- **Draw arrows to show the directions of the forces.**
- **Write what causes each force.**

Causes of forces _____

Causes of forces _____

Causes of forces _____

Causes of forces _____

Causes of forces _____

Causes of forces _____

Now try this!

- **Draw and write about another force you know.**

Teachers' note The children should first have completed page 43. Ask them to demonstrate the forces that act on an elastic band when something is suspended from it and when the object is removed. Remind them that gravity pulls the elastic band towards the Earth even when there is nothing hanging from it. Ask them about other forces they have experienced and remind them of their previous learning about springs and magnets.

Developing Science
Year 6
© A & C Black

Floating forces

Recognise that water exerts an upthrust on a submerged object

• **Weigh each object using a forcemeter ...**

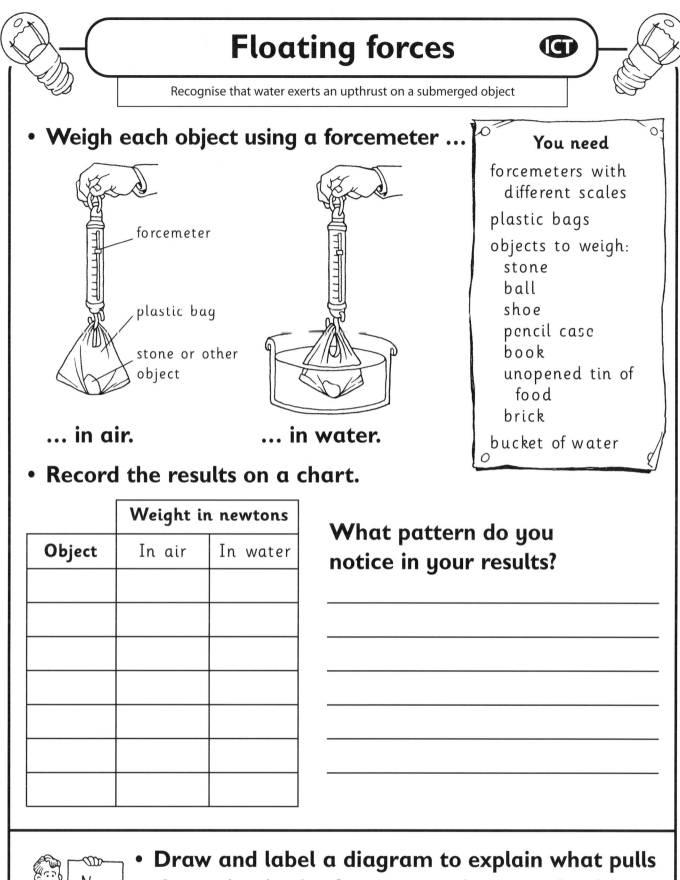

forcemeter

plastic bag

stone or other object

... in air.

... in water.

You need

forcemeters with
 different scales
plastic bags
objects to weigh:
 stone
 ball
 shoe
 pencil case
 book
 unopened tin of
  food
 brick
bucket of water

• **Record the results on a chart.**

Object	Weight in newtons	
	In air	In water

What pattern do you notice in your results?

_____

_____

_____

_____

_____

_____

Now try this!

• **Draw and label a diagram to explain what pulls the spring in the forcemeter downwards when you weigh an object.**

• **Draw another diagram to explain what makes this pull smaller when the object is in water.**

Teachers' note The children should first have completed pages 42–44. Allow the children to feel the upthrust of water by pushing inflated balloons or table tennis balls under water. Ask them about their experiences in swimming pools (pushing armbands and floats under water and feeling them spring up). Remind them of this when they weigh objects in water. See also page 46.

**Developing Science
Year 6
© A & C Black**

Repeat measurements in order to check them

Work in a group.

- **Each weigh the same object, in water, using a different forcemeter, three times.**

- **Without comparing, record your results.**

- **Plot your results on a bar chart:**

You need

a forcemeter each
an object to weigh

Each plot your results in a different colour.

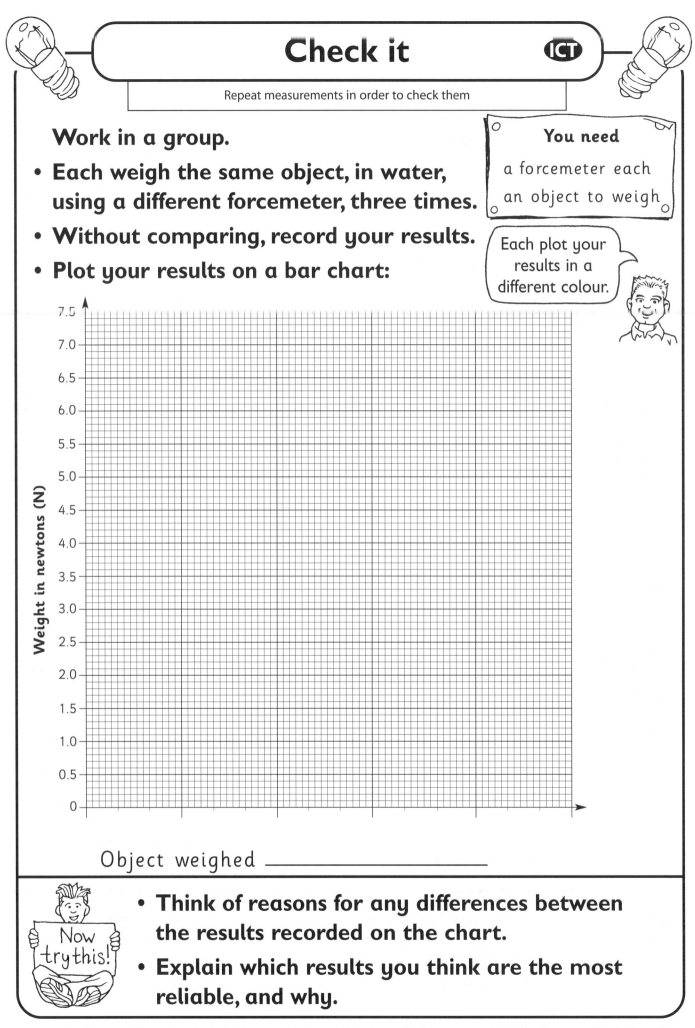

Weight in newtons (N)

7.5
7.0
6.5
6.0
5.5
5.0
4.5
4.0
3.5
3.0
2.5
2.0
1.5
1.0
0.5
0

Object weighed _____

Now try this!

- **Think of reasons for any differences between the results recorded on the chart.**

- **Explain which results you think are the most reliable, and why.**

Teachers' note The children should first have completed pages 42–45. Begin with the results recorded during the activity on page 45. Ask the children why some of them have different results for the same object. Discuss the reliability of forcemeters, whether the children have read them carefully enough and so on.

**Developing Science
Year 6**
© A & C Black

It's elastic

Understand that an elastic band's stretch depends on the force acting on it

- **Measure the length of an elastic band.**
- **Hang weights from it and measure its length each time you add a weight.**
- **Record your results on a line graph.**

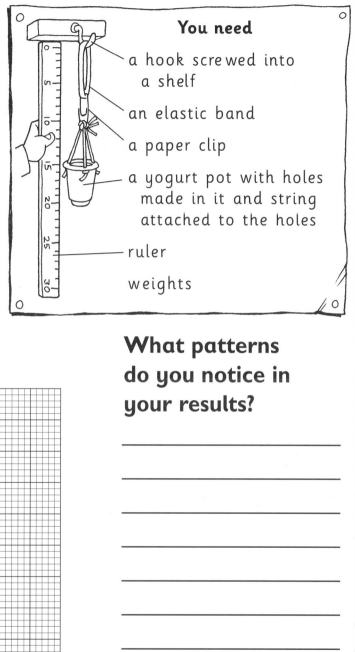

You need

- a hook screwed into a shelf
- an elastic band
- a paper clip
- a yogurt pot with holes made in it and string attached to the holes
- ruler
- weights

⚠️ **Stretched elastic bands can hurt you if they flick back. Heavy weights can hurt your feet if dropped.**

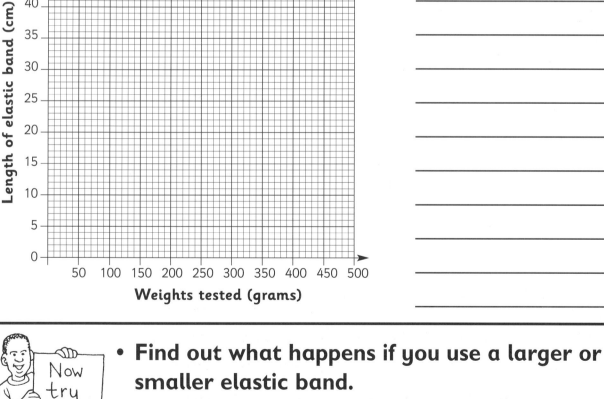

What patterns do you notice in your results?

_____

_____

_____

_____

_____

_____

_____

_____

_____

- **Find out what happens if you use a larger or smaller elastic band.**

Do you find the same patterns in your results?

Teachers' note Revise the children's previous learning about the effect of gravity. They should be able to predict what will happen as they add heavier weights to the elastic band.

Developing Science
Year 6
© A & C Black

Air force

Find out if changing the size of a piece of paper affects how quickly it falls.

- **Fold a piece of paper in half. Label it A.**
- **Fold another piece in the same way and then fold it in half again. Label it B.**
- **Continue in the same way until you have folded all five pieces of paper.**

You need

5 pieces of A4 paper

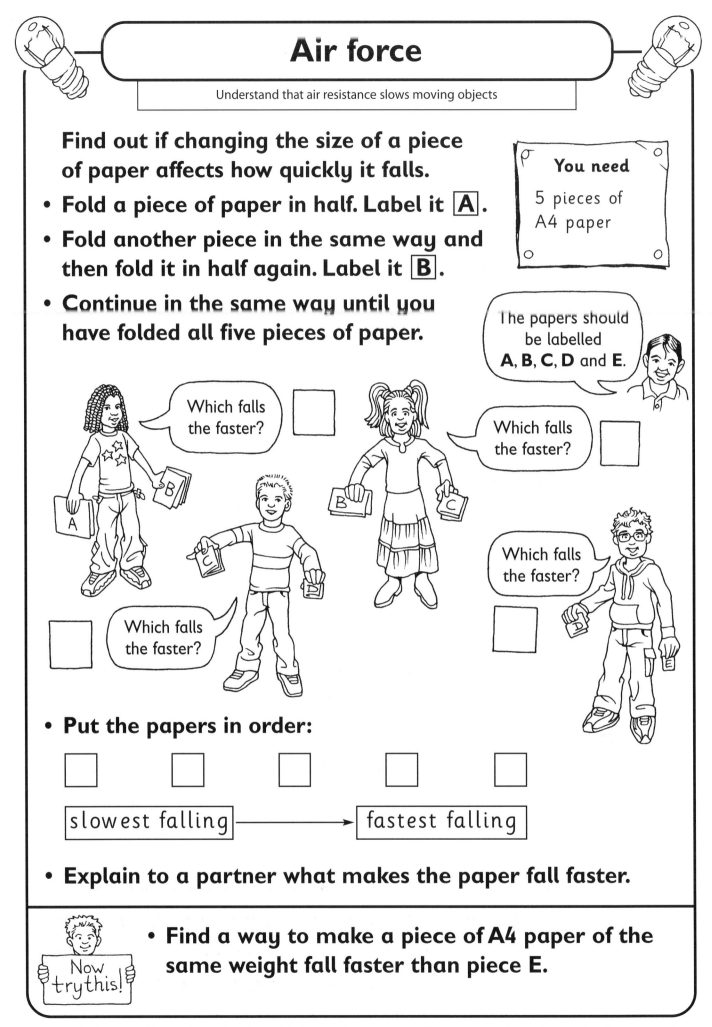

The papers should be labelled **A, B, C, D** and **E**.

Which falls the faster?

Which falls the faster?

Which falls the faster?

Which falls the faster?

- **Put the papers in order:**

slowest falling ⟶ fastest falling

- **Explain to a partner what makes the paper fall faster.**

Now try this!

- **Find a way to make a piece of A4 paper of the same weight fall faster than piece E.**

Teachers' note After the children have dropped the first two pieces of paper, ask them to suggest what made them fall differently. Stress that they are the same weight. Ask what force pulls the paper downwards (gravity) and what force acts upwards to push against gravity, thus slowing down the fall of the paper (air resistance).

Developing Science
Year 6
© A & C Black

Beam blocker

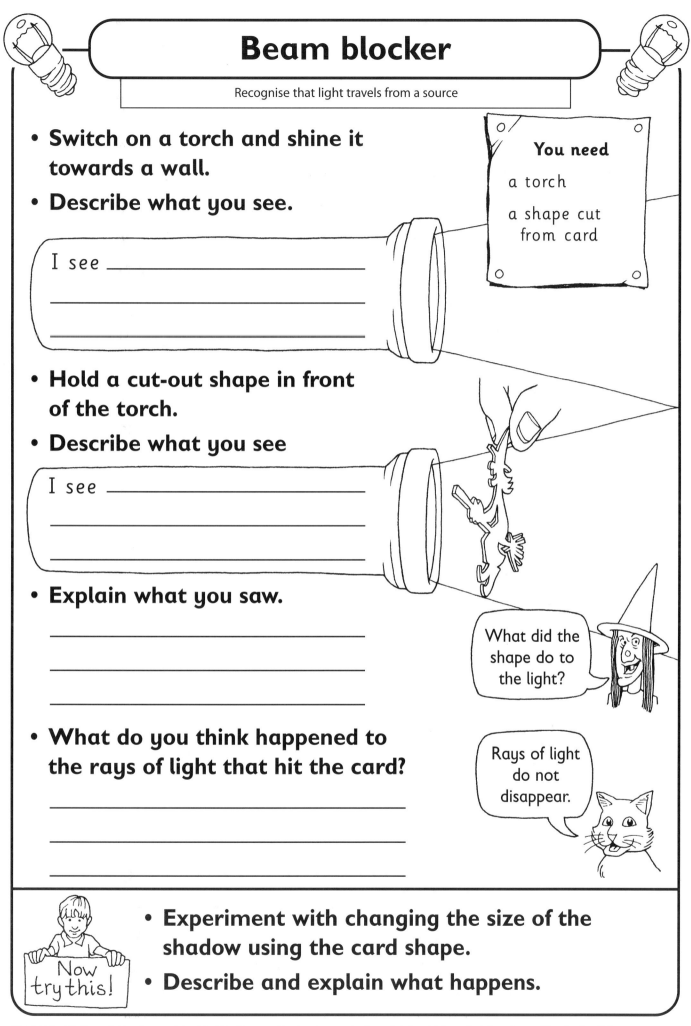

- **Switch on a torch and shine it towards a wall.**
- **Describe what you see.**

I see _____

_____

_____

You need

a torch

a shape cut from card

- **Hold a cut-out shape in front of the torch.**
- **Describe what you see**

I see _____

_____

_____

- **Explain what you saw.**

_____

_____

_____

What did the shape do to the light?

- **What do you think happened to the rays of light that hit the card?**

_____

_____

_____

Rays of light do not disappear.

Now try this!

- **Experiment with changing the size of the shadow using the card shape.**
- **Describe and explain what happens.**

Teachers' note Powerful torches work best for this; they usually give sharper shadows. Ask the children what stops the light from the torch reaching the wall. Where does that light go to? (Most of it is absorbed if the broomstick rider is cut from dark paper; some is reflected, especially if the paper is light.) Revise the term *opaque* for materials that do not let light through and so create shadows.

Developing Science
Year 6
© A & C Black

Now you see it

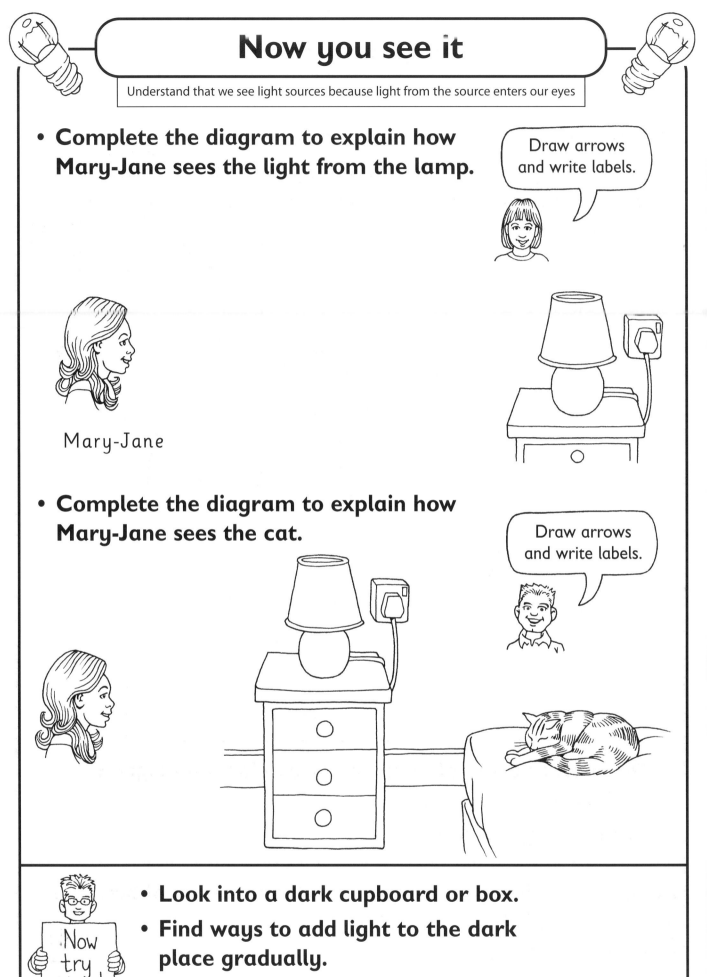

- Complete the diagram to explain how Mary-Jane sees the light from the lamp.

Draw arrows and write labels.

Mary-Jane

- Complete the diagram to explain how Mary-Jane sees the cat.

Draw arrows and write labels.

Now try this!

- Look into a dark cupboard or box.
- Find ways to add light to the dark place gradually.
- Describe and explain what you see.

Teachers' note Use this page to assess the children's understanding about how light helps us to see things. Encourage them to share their ideas about how we see light from a lamp, and provide information books about the eye to show that the pupil of the eye is a hole that lets in light.

Developing Science
Year 6
© A & C Black

Target practice

Recognise that light from an object can be reflected by a mirror

- **Cut out the target and fix it onto a wall.**
- **Find a way to make a beam of light from a torch hit the target without shining the torch towards it.**

Keep the rest of the page.

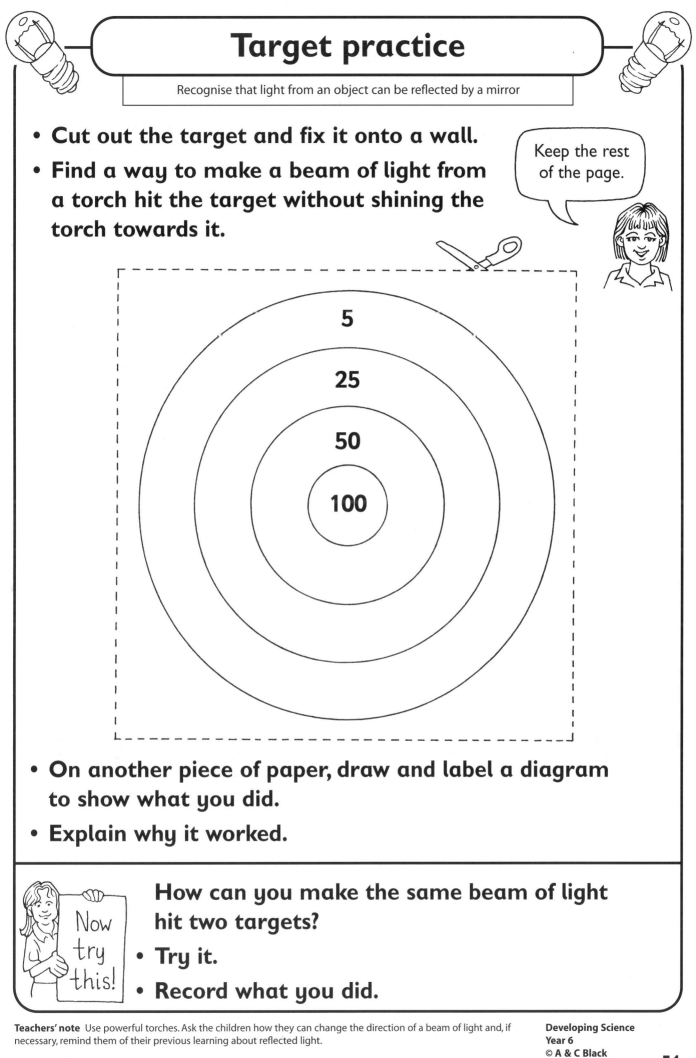

5

25

50

100

- **On another piece of paper, draw and label a diagram to show what you did.**
- **Explain why it worked.**

Now try this!

How can you make the same beam of light hit two targets?

- **Try it.**
- **Record what you did.**

Teachers' note Use powerful torches. Ask the children how they can change the direction of a beam of light and, if necessary, remind them of their previous learning about reflected light.

Developing Science
Year 6
© A & C Black

51

Beam tracer

Indicate the direction of a beam by a straight line with an arrowhead

- **Predict where each beam of light will go. Draw a line with an arrowhead to show your prediction.**

- **Switch on the light box or torch to check. Draw this beam in another colour.**

Use a ruler.

You need

light box*

slit

6 volt battery

mirror

bulldog clips to hold mirror

* You could use a powerful torch and a piece of card with a slit cut in it.

Predictions and results

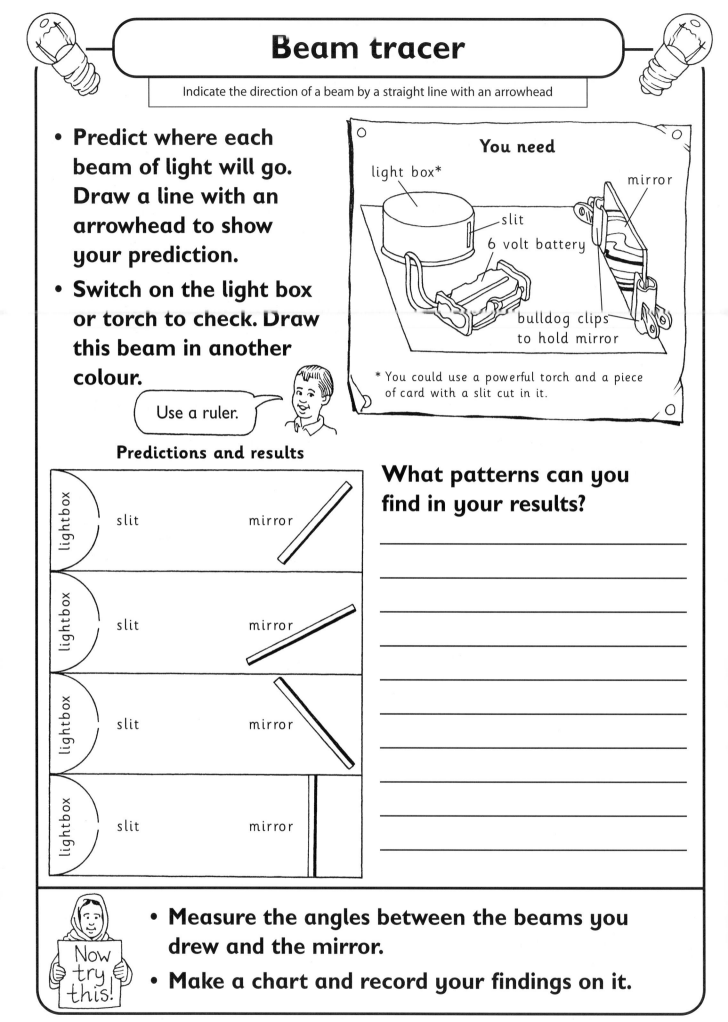

lightbox	slit	mirror
lightbox	slit	mirror
lightbox	slit	mirror
lightbox	slit	mirror

What patterns can you find in your results?

_____

_____

_____

_____

_____

_____

_____

_____

_____

_____

_____

_____

Now try this!

- **Measure the angles between the beams you drew and the mirror.**

- **Make a chart and record your findings on it.**

Teachers' note The children should first have completed page 51. A bright light works best for this activity. Remind the children about how they aimed the torch beam at the target; the angle of the mirror was important.

Developing Science
Year 6
© A & C Black

Enlarge it

- **Cut out the butterflies and glue them onto card.**
- **Stand up the large one like this:**

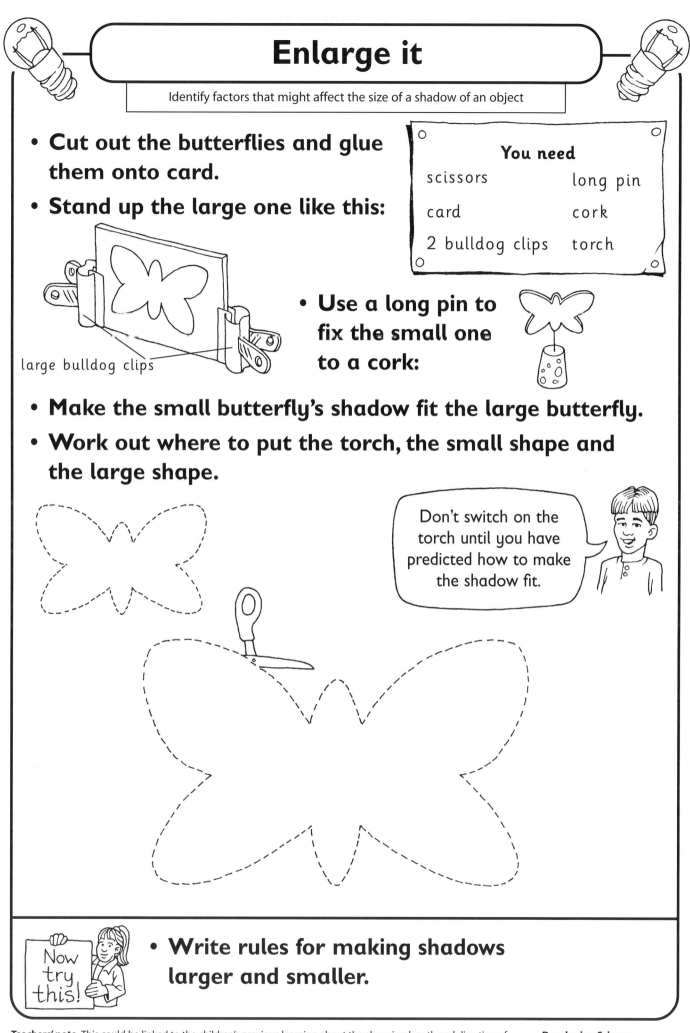

large bulldog clips

You need

scissors	long pin
card	cork
2 bulldog clips	torch

- **Use a long pin to fix the small one to a cork:**

- **Make the small butterfly's shadow fit the large butterfly.**
- **Work out where to put the torch, the small shape and the large shape.**

Don't switch on the torch until you have predicted how to make the shadow fit.

Now try this!

- **Write rules for making shadows larger and smaller.**

Teachers' note This could be linked to the children's previous learning about the changing length and direction of shadows cast by objects in the sunshine: the position of the Sun affects the size and direction of the shadows.

Developing Science
Year 6
© A & C Black

Shadows and reflections

Recognise the difference between shadows and 'reflections'

• **Cut out the cards and divide them into two sets:**

True and **False**

A shadow is a black reflection.	A shadow is a place where there is no light.	A reflection is the same as a shadow.	Light-coloured materials reflect more light than dark ones.
We have shadows only when it is sunny.	Opaque materials do not let light through.	Only opaque materials reflect light.	Only transparent materials reflect light.
When light is reflected it changes direction.	We can see bright things only because other things do not reflect light.	We see light because it is bright.	We see light because it enters our eyes.
Your shadow is reflected in the mirror.	A reflection is made when something blocks out light.	Shadows are made when light is blocked.	Light travels in a straight line from a source such as a torch until something stops it.

Teachers' note The children should first have completed pages 49–53. Use this page to review what the children have learned during the work in this section; this helps them to take an active part in their own learning. They could work individually or in groups.

**Developing Science
Year 6**
© A & C Black

Who's there?

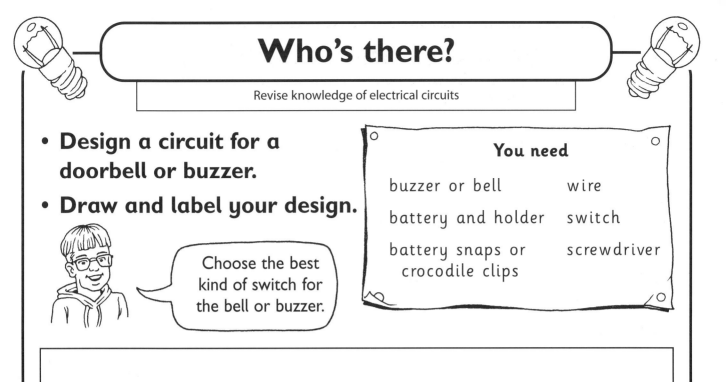

- **Design a circuit for a doorbell or buzzer.**
- **Draw and label your design.**

Choose the best kind of switch for the bell or buzzer.

You need

buzzer or bell   wire

battery and holder   switch

battery snaps or   screwdriver
crocodile clips

- **Make and test your circuit.**

  How well did it work?

  _____

  _____

  _____

  What improvements can you make?

  _____

  _____

  _____

Now try this!

- **Find a way to add a bulb to the circuit that lights up when the switch is pressed.**

Teachers' note Ask the children if they can remember the most important points about an electrical circuit. Draw out the need for it to be unbroken. Also remind them that batteries need to give the right amount of power for the things they are meant to work. The children could try different batteries for their bell or buzzer until they find one strong enough. In the extension activity, a parallel circuit should be used (see pages 12 and 57).

Developing Science
Year 6
© **A & C Black**

Circuit diagrams

- **Draw a picture of each circuit.**
- **Predict: will they work?**
- **Make the circuits and test them.**
- **Record what happens.**

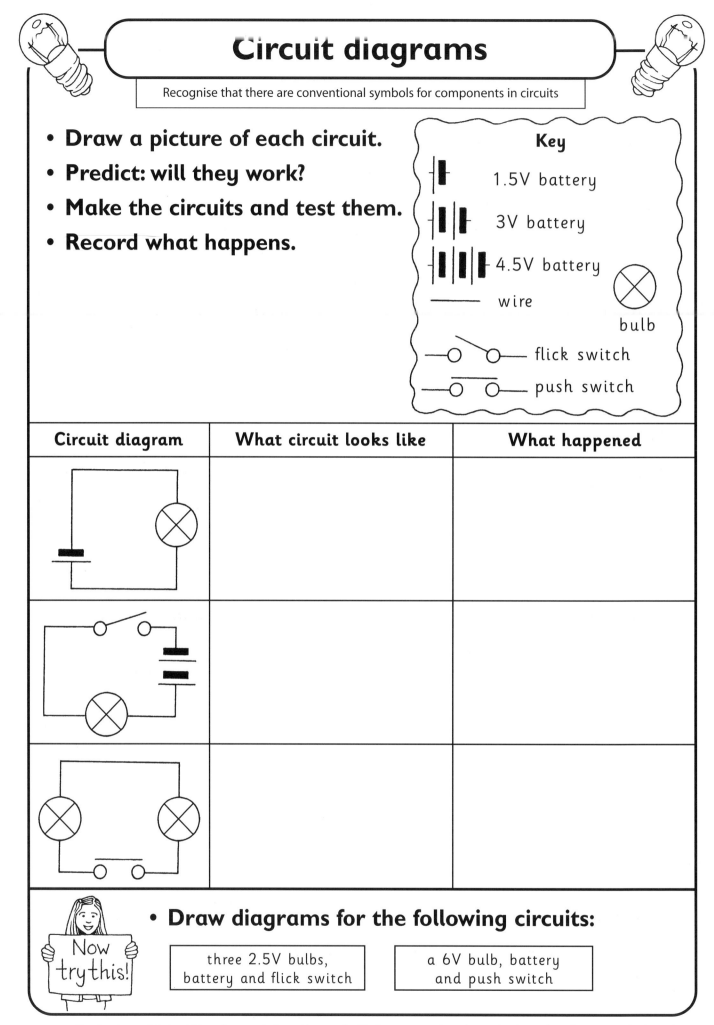

Key

- 1.5V battery
- 3V battery
- 4.5V battery
- wire
- bulb
- flick switch
- push switch

Circuit diagram	What circuit looks like	What happened

- **Draw diagrams for the following circuits:**

three 2.5V bulbs, battery and flick switch	a 6V bulb, battery and push switch

Now try this!

Teachers' note Ask the children about symbols used in everyday life that most people understand without a key. Also talk about symbols used by groups of people that might not be understood by others (such as map symbols). Introduce and explain the symbols in the key on this page. Some children might be able to work out how to draw symbols for other batteries (for example, 6V, 9V or 12V).

Developing Science
Year 6
© **A & C Black**

Wired up

Understand that the brightness of bulbs in a circuit can be changed

The four main rooms in this doll's house need lights.

- **On this picture, draw and label the circuit you will make. You could put the battery in the kitchen cupboard.**

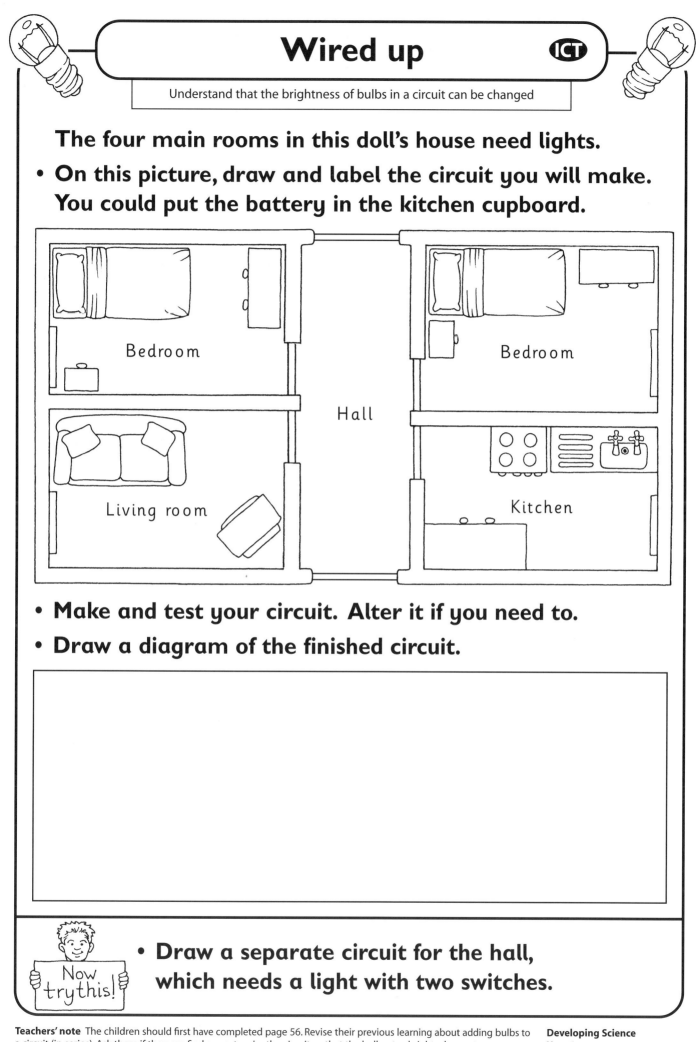

- **Make and test your circuit. Alter it if you need to.**
- **Draw a diagram of the finished circuit.**

Now try this!

- **Draw a separate circuit for the hall, which needs a light with two switches.**

Teachers' note The children should first have completed page 56. Revise their previous learning about adding bulbs to a circuit (in series). Ask them if they can find a way to wire the circuit so that the bulbs stay bright when extra ones are added (a parallel circuit – see page 12).

Developing Science
Year 6
© **A & C Black**

Wire wise

Understand that the brightness of bulbs can be changed by changing the wires

- **Look at different kinds of wire. Notice what they are used for.**
- **Draw, label and describe the wires:**

You need

different types of electrical wire:

wire used in mains

single-strand steel wire

cotton covered single-strand wire

fuse wire

plastic-coated wire

flexes

⚠ **Never experiment with mains electricity.**

- **List the wires in order.**

thinnest wire ⟶ thickest wire

- **Find out if the thickness of a wire affects the brightness of a bulb.**
- **Record your results on a separate piece of paper.**

Now try this!
- **Find out why some circuits need thicker wire than others.**

Teachers' note If possible, invite an electrician to talk to the children about his or her work, to show them different kinds of wire and to explain how they are used in circuits and for what purposes.

Developing Science
Year 6
© **A & C Black**

Dim it

- **Join the wires to close the gap in the circuit.**
- **Measure the brightness of the bulb:**

  It could be seen through

  [ ] sheets of paper.

- **Put the pencil in the gap and measure the brightness of the bulb.**

  [ ] sheets of paper

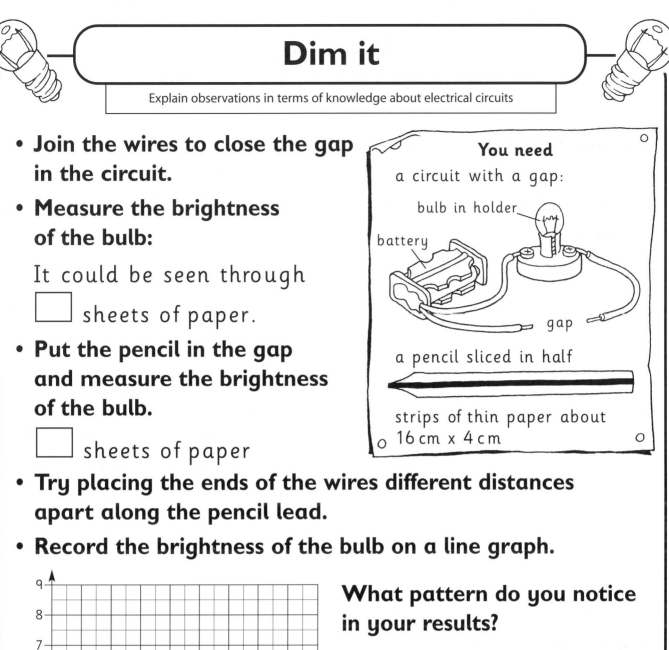

You need

a circuit with a gap:

bulb in holder

battery

gap

a pencil sliced in half

strips of thin paper about 16 cm x 4 cm

- **Try placing the ends of the wires different distances apart along the pencil lead.**
- **Record the brightness of the bulb on a line graph.**

What pattern do you notice in your results?

_____

_____

_____

_____

_____

_____

_____

_____

[Line graph: y-axis labelled "Sheets of paper" from 0 to 9; x-axis labelled "Distance between wires (cm)" from 0 to 18]

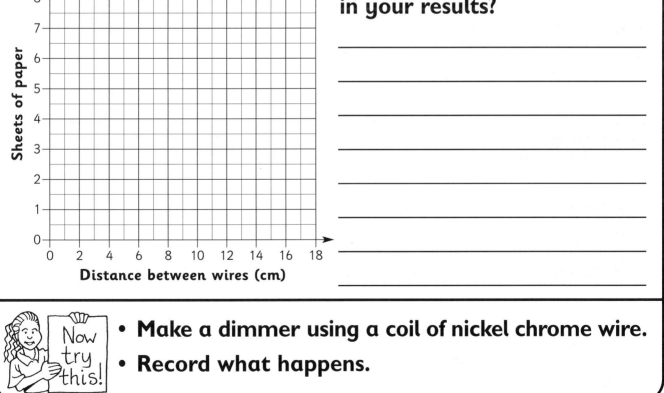

- **Make a dimmer using a coil of nickel chrome wire.**
- **Record what happens.**

Teachers' note Show the children a disconnected domestic dimmer switch and let them examine the inside. Tell them that it can alter the power going to the bulb, making the bulb brighter or dimmer (or switching it on and off). Remind them of their previous work on conductors and resistors and tell them that some materials conduct electricity better than others.

Developing Science
Year 6
© A & C Black

Tilt switch

- ## Make a tilt switch like this:

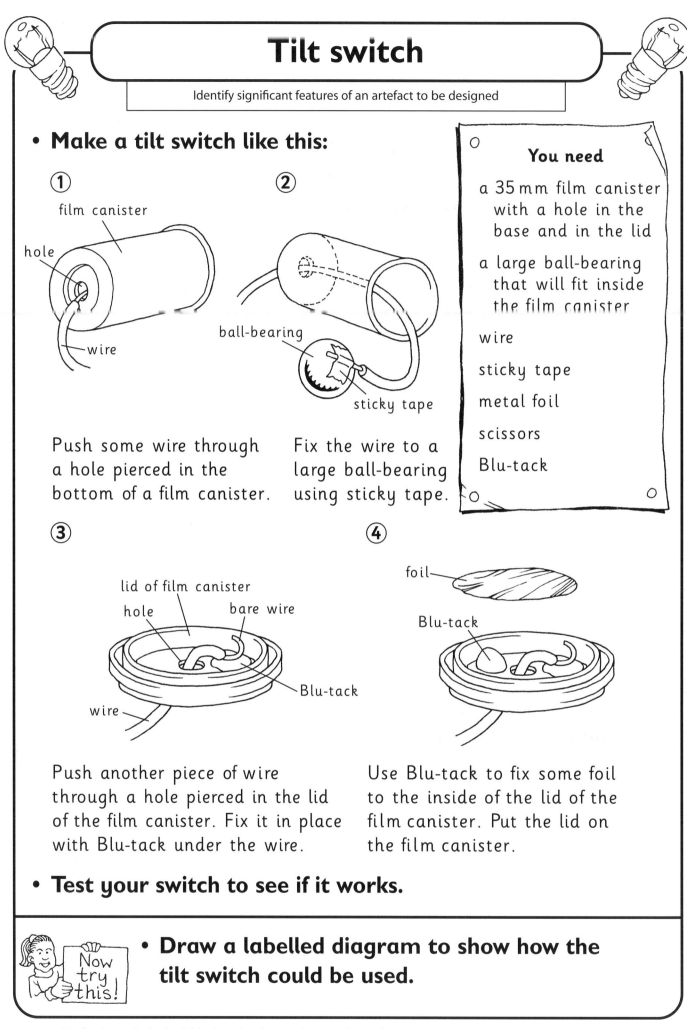

① film canister
hole
wire

Push some wire through a hole pierced in the bottom of a film canister.

② ball-bearing
sticky tape

Fix the wire to a large ball-bearing using sticky tape.

You need

a 35 mm film canister with a hole in the base and in the lid

a large ball-bearing that will fit inside the film canister

wire

sticky tape

metal foil

scissors

Blu-tack

③ lid of film canister
hole
bare wire
Blu-tack
wire

Push another piece of wire through a hole pierced in the lid of the film canister. Fix it in place with Blu-tack under the wire.

④ foil
Blu-tack

Use Blu-tack to fix some foil to the inside of the lid of the film canister. Put the lid on the film canister.

- ## Test your switch to see if it works.

Now try this!

- ## Draw a labelled diagram to show how the tilt switch could be used.

Teachers' note Revise the children's previous learning about switches in electrical circuits. Ask them what a switch is for (to join or break a circuit to make a component work or to stop it working). Provide some materials for making switches and discuss the ways in which they can be joined in order to create a metal path for electricity to follow and to break this path when necessary.

Developing Science
Year 6
© **A & C Black**

Alarm

- **Plan a circuit for an alarm that will go off if someone takes away the television.**
- **Draw and label your ideas.**

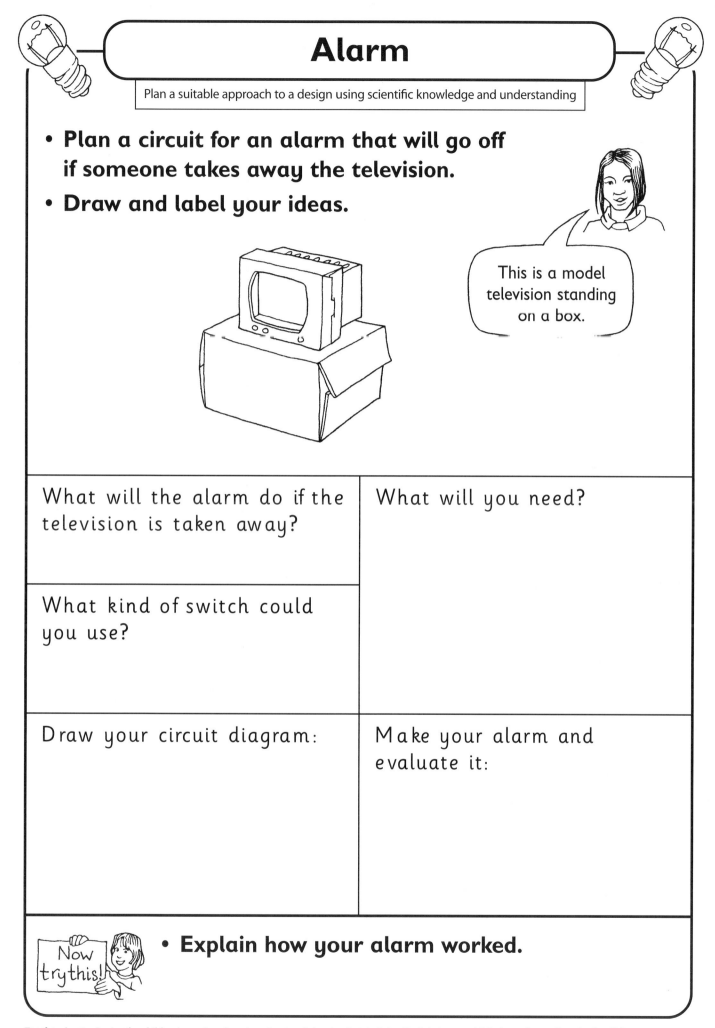

This is a model television standing on a box.

What will the alarm do if the television is taken away?	What will you need?
What kind of switch could you use?	
Draw your circuit diagram:	Make your alarm and evaluate it:

Now try this!

- **Explain how your alarm worked.**

Teachers' note Revise the children's previous learning about switches in electrical circuits. Ask them to think about the ways in which switches are operated and which would be the most suitable for the context. If necessary, stress that the television will be lifted and tilted if it is stolen.

Developing Science
Year 6
© A & C Black

61

Pressure pad

- **Design a switch that can be hidden under a mat so that it switches on an alarm when someone steps on the mat.**

My switch:

Circuit using the switch:

Labelled drawing | Circuit diagram

- **Explain how the switch will work.**

Teachers' note Revise the children's previous learning about switches in electrical circuits. (Show them a piece of folded card that works like a hinge and ask them if it could be used as a switch.) Stress the need for a continuous metal path and ask them how they could incorporate this into their switch. Demonstrate how foam pads squash when depressed and discuss how these could be used in making a switch.

Developing Science
Year 6
© A & C Black

62

Switch test

Test and explain designs using scientific knowledge and understanding

- **Plan a trial for your pressure pad switch.**

How I shall test the switch:

Draw and label a diagram.

Evaluation

What worked well:

What needs to be changed:

- **Change one part of the switch at a time.**
- **Write about what you changed and what happened.**

Now try this!

- **Set up the switch in a circuit where it will be used.**

Teachers' note This could be used with page 64. Encourage the children to state what their switch should do if it is to work effectively. Does it do that? How well? What could be improved? What could the children try in order to improve the switch? Encourage them to change one thing at a time and observe the results.

Developing Science
Year 6
© **A & C Black**

Trial log

Put your design on trial.

- **Use this page to log your results as you test something you have designed and made.**

Item to be tested:

Expected result:

Actual result:

Component to be changed:

Change 1	Result
Change 2	Result
Change 3	Result
Change 4	Result

- **Draw and describe how you can improve the item. Does any other component need to be changed?**
- **Use another chart to record the changes.**

Teachers' note This could be used to help the children to plan a methodical and well-organised evaluation and modification of the switches and burglar alarms they have made, or of any other artefacts they make.

Developing Science
Year 6
© A & C Black